CONVERSATIONS WITH **YOUR FINANCIAL THERAPIST**

CONVERSATIONS WITH **YOUR FINANCIAL THERAPIST**

STORIES AND SCRIPTS TO GROW YOUR MONEY MINDSET

ERIKA WASSERMAN, CFT

WILEY

Copyright © 2025 by John Wiley & Sons, Inc. All rights reserved, including rights for text and data mining and training of artificial technologies or similar technologies.

Published by John Wiley & Sons, Inc., Hoboken, New Jersey.
Published simultaneously in Canada.

No part of this publication may be reproduced, stored in a retrieval system, or transmitted in any form or by any means, electronic, mechanical, photocopying, recording, scanning, or otherwise, except as permitted under Section 107 or 108 of the 1976 United States Copyright Act, without either the prior written permission of the Publisher, or authorization through payment of the appropriate per-copy fee to the Copyright Clearance Center, Inc., 222 Rosewood Drive, Danvers, MA 01923, (978) 750-8400, fax (978) 750-4470, or on the web at www.copyright.com. Requests to the Publisher for permission should be addressed to the Permissions Department, John Wiley & Sons, Inc., 111 River Street, Hoboken, NJ 07030, (201) 748-6011, fax (201) 748-6008, or online at http://www.wiley .com/go/permission.

Trademarks: Wiley and the Wiley logo are trademarks or registered trademarks of John Wiley & Sons, Inc. and/or its affiliates in the United States and other countries and may not be used without written permission. All other trademarks are the property of their respective owners. John Wiley & Sons, Inc. is not associated with any product or vendor mentioned in this book.

Limit of Liability/Disclaimer of Warranty: While the publisher and author have used their best efforts in preparing this book, they make no representations or warranties with respect to the accuracy or completeness of the contents of this book and specifically disclaim any implied warranties of merchantability or fitness for a particular purpose. No warranty may be created or extended by sales representatives or written sales materials. The advice and strategies contained herein may not be suitable for your situation. You should consult with a professional where appropriate. Further, readers should be aware that websites listed in this work may have changed or disappeared between when this work was written and when it is read. Neither the publisher nor authors shall be liable for any loss of profit or any other commercial damages, including but not limited to special, incidental, consequential, or other damages.

For general information on our other products and services or for technical support, please contact our Customer Care Department within the United States at (800) 762-2974, outside the United States at (317) 572-3993 or fax (317) 572-4002.

Wiley also publishes its books in a variety of electronic formats. Some content that appears in print may not be available in electronic formats. For more information about Wiley products, visit our web site at www.wiley.com.

Library of Congress Cataloging-in-Publication Data is Available:

ISBN 9781394303854 (Cloth)
ISBN 9781394303861 (ePub)
ISBN 9781394303847 (ePDF)

Cover Design: Wiley
Cover Image: Courtesy of Author
Author Photo: © Daniel Wakefield

SKY10122837_072425

To the man who offered endless unsolicited advice because he didn't have that kind of guidance growing up. Your wisdom gave me the confidence to talk authentically about the power of money, the courage to write this book, and the belief in humanity's ability to do extraordinary things.

What I wouldn't give for just one more conversation with you.
I love you, Dad.
Louis Wasserman 1946–2017

Dear Reader,

You are cordially invited to keep this conversation going with instant access to chapter insights, bonus scripts, and more!

Go to

www.c-yft.com/book to stay in touch

Sincerely,

Erika

Erika Wasserman
Your Financial Therapist
www.yourfinancialtherapist.com
www.c-yft.com
Instagram: /Yourfinancialtherapist
LinkedIn: /Yourfinancialtherapist

CONTENTS

INTRODUCTION 1

CHAPTER 1
THE MONEY MINDSET METHOD: YOUR GUIDE TO
FINANCIAL CLARITY 11

CHAPTER 2
WELCOME TO ADULTHOOD: WHERE FINANCIAL
FREEDOM MEETS CONFUSION 19

CHAPTER 3
FROM BURNOUT TO BREAKTHROUGH: TAKING
CHARGE OF YOUR CAREER 39

CHAPTER 4
MERGING MONEY AND MINDSETS WITH A LOVER 55

CHAPTER 5
FROM DIAPERS TO DOG HAIR: THE OVERWHELMING JOY
(AND EXPENSE) OF GROWING YOUR FAMILY 89

CHAPTER 6
FROM OURS TO MINE: FINDING STABILITY IN
FINANCIAL SEPARATION 105

CONTENTS

CHAPTER 7
    RAISING TOGETHER, APART: CO-PARENTING WITH
    FINANCIAL CONFIDENCE   125

CHAPTER 8
    ROLE REVERSAL: NAVIGATING FINANCES WITH AGING PARENTS   141

CHAPTER 9
    LAST WISHES AND LOOSE ENDS: ESTATE PLANNING REALITIES   159

CHAPTER 10
    PARENTING DOESN'T END AT 18: NAVIGATING
    THE NEXT CHAPTER WITH ADULT CHILDREN   179

BONUS CHAPTER
HIRING AND FIRING A FINANCIAL ADVISOR   193

CONCLUSION
OWN IT: YOUR RELATIONSHIP WITH MONEY ONE
CONVERSATION AT A TIME   209

SCRIPTS   213

APPENDIX: CHARACTER OVERVIEWS   263

NOTES   267

ACKNOWLEDGMENTS   271

ABOUT THE AUTHOR   275

INDEX   277

Mindset, noun

A person's way of thinking and their opinions.

Money mindset, noun

A person's way of thinking and attitudes toward money. It shapes your decisions on how you save, spend, and manage your finances.

CONVERSATIONS WITH **YOUR FINANCIAL THERAPIST**

INTRODUCTION

et's go for a ride . . . on a roller-coaster ride . . . of life. Buckle up!
Welcome to *Conversations with Your Financial Therapist*. I am glad you are here. Talking about money is often considered a taboo topic, done behind closed doors in secret—or not at all. The fact that you are here ready and willing to learn more about how to have productive conversations is a great start; you are ahead of most. Having money conversations is often a new skill for my clients, one that needs practice like any new hobby or habit.

I often walk around neighborhoods thinking, "What's going on behind those walls?" Well now you will get a look inside within the pages of this book. I wrote this book to give you a sneak peek behind the scenes as if you were sitting inside people's homes. You will be introduced to seven main characters, travel through life milestones with them, and have insights into their conversations, leaving you with detailed scripts you can reference for your own conversations.

This book was written for you, real people with real-life problems, wanting to get healthier with their relationships with money but not sure where to begin.

Our money beliefs come from three main areas of our lives: our background and how money was talked about, or not talked about, growing up; religious messaging and culture; and our own personal experiences.

By young adulthood, we usually find ourselves in a fixed mindset based on these three pillars and stop growing, learning, and expanding our financial mindset.

Like any healthy relationship, it starts with a conversation, story sharing, and building trust. So before we begin this journey together, please allow me the opportunity to share a little about me with a story (or two) to gain insights on me, Your Financial Therapist.

Sitting in the backseat of the car, a quick trip to the store with my dad usually started with a math lesson. "How much would one can of beans cost if the sale was two for $0.99?" The quizzing would progress throughout the drive and would continue at the checkout counter when it was time to pay the grocery bill. My dad would take out the dollar bills and jiggle the coins in his hand and ask me to pay the bill, ask me what the return change would be. If he was in a good mood, I could keep the returned coins. You can see, money conversations were all around me starting very young and continued throughout my journey in life. *Is life a journey* or is it more of a roller-coaster ride of life? My vote is life is more of a roller-coaster ride. Some things make me want to throw my hands up and scream with excitement and other times the twists and turns are jolting, and ones that make my stomach drop like when my dad died unexpectedly in 2017.

Money and emotions are tied together so closely. I can still recall early childhood memories of a great aunt slipping me $5 for ice cream money at family events or of my turquoise piggy bank that I stashed my cash in as a kid feeling good that I had savings, opportunities if I wanted to buy something myself, or being proud when I was the one my parents came to when they needed cash and knew I kept a stash in my little bank. All of these small moments helped shape my relationship with money. Just like your unique moments in life have shaped yours.

My love for numbers continued with me on my roller coaster to college. I graduated with a degree in finance, began working for IBM Global Services, where I would grow both my career and family. I met a boyfriend

Introduction

who became a husband, father to my three kids, then ended up an ex-husband who now is my co-parent. Along the way, IBM lived up to its acronym for "I've Been Moved" and we moved nine times in just over a decade including living in three countries (United States, Japan, and China). In this span of time I did everything from merging money with a new partner, to shifting spending for babies, to opening and closing bank accounts in various countries, buying and selling homes, to navigating a divorce, co-parenting, and the death of my dad, which has made my roller coaster of life quite eventful. Yet all along it was preparing me for where I am today: to support you and others with kindness, empathy, and understanding.

During my divorce, I had three kids under the age of four, I had recently left corporate America to focus on raising kids, and I was working with entrepreneurs part-time helping them grow their businesses. This allowed me more flexibility with my time. But what did that all mean when I could barely get off the floor on some of the early days of the divorce process? I vividly remember one day in particular. I was lying on the floor in our marital home trying to meditate, bring peace and focus into the morning, when my daughters started to crawl over me and ask me what I was doing on the floor. I tried to explain that I was focusing a few minutes before I start my day by asking myself three questions:

- Who am I?
- What do I want?
- What is my purpose?

This led to a conversation (as one can do with a two- and three-year-old and sleeping baby) on what their purpose was for the day as I tried to explain that my purpose was to help others going through challenges, taking the higher road as I was doing now for myself. For me, I was in control of the family finances even though both of us had finance degrees. I was the chief financial officer of the family, which when the world was ripped out from under me also meant I knew what I needed: to not just survive but thrive for my new family dynamic. I had the ability to ask questions, come up with options, and create opportunities for us to think outside the box for our young family. Thankfully my daughters' dad and I were able to negotiate our divorce in three months with a mediator. We both stayed focused on the end goal of supporting and raising good humans. I also know this would not be possible without my confidence in my relationship with money (Thanks, Dad!). The same was true years later when my dad passed away and it was time to step in and support my Mom to build her confidence in money management, an area she hadn't been responsible for in her 50 years of marriage.

Those dark days over a decade ago played a big part in defining my purpose. I realized that I could help people take the higher road when life gets complicated, but at the same time I didn't know how until the day I heard the term *financial therapist*. I still recall the moment I heard the term and the world stopped for me. This was it! I felt like I was transported back to those days of lying on the floor trying to figure out my purpose and here it was, right in front of me a decade later. Chills ran through my body. I immediately enrolled at Kansas State University program for a graduate certificate in financial therapy under the profound leadership of Dr. Megan McCoy, then became the 15th person in the world to be certified in this field through the Financial Therapy Association. Currently there are 100 CFTs (Certified Financial Therapists) and the number is growing each year.

Today, I run a thriving business as a global speaker and financial wellness expert on this topic, helping individuals and organizations navigate the emotional and practical sides of money, guiding people to healthier lives, creating more productive and focused employees, and wealthier individuals. My journey has taken me from corporate stages around the world to intimate one-on-one client sessions, where I guide people toward financial empowerment and healthier money relationships. "Let's Talk Finances Conversation Cards" (available on Amazon) were created and

Introduction

designed to foster meaningful financial conversations at home, shifting the narrative about money from one of stress to understanding. Whether I'm presenting to a room of executives, working with couples to align their financial goals, or helping someone rebuild their confidence after a life change, my mission remains clear: to support people in creating a life they can say yes to confidently including their finances. This book is an extension of that mission, and I'm honored to be on this journey with you.

Welcome to a new chapter of clarity, confidence, and growth in your financial life!

CONVERSATIONS WITH YOUR FINANCIAL THERAPIST

10 REASONS TO GROW YOUR FINANCIAL MINDSET

- **Improved financial management:** Developing a healthy money mindset helps you create and stick to budgets, track spending, and manage debt more effectively.
- **Increased savings:** A positive money mindset encourages you to prioritize saving, build an emergency fund, and invest for the future.
- **Better spending habits:** You become more mindful of your purchases, avoiding impulsive spending and making thoughtful financial decisions.
- **Enhanced financial security:** With better management and savings, you gain a sense of financial security, reducing stress and anxiety about money.
- **Achieving financial goals:** A strong money mindset helps you set clear financial goals and create actionable plans to achieve them.
- **Greater wealth accumulation:** By investing wisely and managing money well, you can grow your wealth over time and build a solid financial foundation.
- **Reduced financial stress:** Understanding and controlling your finances can significantly lower the stress and worry associated with money.
- **Increased financial confidence:** As you become more knowledgeable and skilled in managing money, your confidence in making financial decisions grows.
- **Better relationships:** A healthy money mindset promotes open communication about finances with partners, family, and friends, leading to stronger, more supportive relationships.
- **Improved overall well-being:** Financial stability and reduced stress contribute to better mental, emotional, and physical health, enhancing your overall quality of life.

Introduction

MEET THE CAST

Throughout the book, we'll be navigating life's financial ups and downs with the help of some friends. These characters will share their own stories, challenges, and solutions as they tackle major life events they experience—from car repairs to managing relationships, debts, and everything in between, these stories are a blend of what I have seen with many of my clients. You might even see a little of yourself in a few of them.

Here are the voices you'll be hearing along the way:

Averi

Averi, 30, is a powerhouse of ambition and resilience. Raised in a household where she bounced between her divorced parents, she swore never to repeat that pattern with her own kids. She graduated at the top of her class, played college basketball on a scholarship, and pursued law school, despite the student loan debt that came with it. Averi went through years of horrible stomach issues with no answers as to what it was until being diagnosed with Crohn's disease. She's a dedicated lawyer working 60-hour weeks and trying to balance her health. A few months ago, she met Sam on a dating app, and together they're navigating financial hurdles, from vacation costs to student loans. Averi balances her demanding career with the excitement of a new relationship, thoughtfully preparing for future expenses and navigating life with determination and grace.

Gabe

Gabe, 22, is diving headfirst into the world of consulting for a top international firm with the finesse of a caffeinated dolphin. Top of his class? Check. The ability to study for hours? Absolutely! But now, he is navigating living alone for the first time in New York City, managing bills, and feeling overwhelmed all while maintaining a job and a budding social life. There aren't enough hours in the day; in the past his parents just paid for everything.

Gabe's nervous about moving into the next phase of life of spreadsheets and street smarts, all while keeping his humor intact.

José

At 19, José's life has shaped him into someone far older, as he's spent years carrying the weight of adult duties to provide for his immigrant parents and two younger siblings. As the family's go-to translator and problem-solver, he is adept at navigating the challenges of their new country. Working as a roofer, José isn't afraid of hard work or long hours, understanding the true value of money from his humble beginnings. His life took a romantic turn when he met Madison during a lunch break in the next town over. Their instant connection marked the beginning of a new chapter, blending love, responsibility, and finances.

Madison

Madison, 19, is the sassy barista extraordinaire at her hometown diner, where she's not just serving up food but also brews dreams of owning the place someday. Despite early challenges in her home life, being bounced around, barely graduating high school, she's found her groove now and is embracing her journey with grit and a contagious optimism. Surrounded by familiar faces and fueled by determination, Madison's story is a testament to resilience and the power of pursuing your passions, even when they get derailed a bit, with a smile and sprinkle of sass.

Sam

Meet Sam, 35, the financial whiz who moved from a small apartment into a dream home with some savvy investing skills. By day, she's the heart and soul of a nonprofit, cheering on youth to conquer life's challenges and build their confidence. Growing up in a rock-solid family with two younger siblings, Sam has always been the go-to leader—both at home and now in her bustling life. With an infectious enthusiasm for life and love, Sam is on a quest for a relationship that's not just equal but downright electric. Early financial moves have set her up for success in real estate. She has the house, but is waiting to make it a home. Sam had not been as successful in the romance world until Averi came along. Sam is determined to keep growing, inspiring, and maybe even surprising herself along the way by finding a way to merge her financial success with a newfound love.

Sophia

Sophia, 24, is a blend of ambition and uncertainty, driven by early morning runs and a fierce determination to thrive in freelancing. Her journey is a mix of laughter, doubt, learning, and tears as she navigates finding her independence. Raised as a latchkey kid—babysat by sitcoms, microwave dinners, and the reality of watching her parents work hard every day—Sophia's resilience stands strong. Especially now when she's living with several roommates while trying to bridge into the adult world. Her story combines humor and bravery, reminding us it's okay to fear the unknown—like signing your first lease.

William

A dedicated marketing manager, 48-year-old William has a calm and easygoing demeanor that reflects the strong values of responsibility and compassion instilled in him by his close-knit family. After a challenging first marriage that failed, William was left with financial trust issues after learning during the divorce process that there was hidden debt. He has uncertainty about ever merging money with anyone ever again. William is a loving father to his two sons, actively participating in their lives. He also has a committed relationship with his new partner, Sophia. Together, they navigate the complexities of blending their lives and finances while eagerly anticipating the potential of a child together.

CHAPTER ONE

THE MONEY MINDSET METHOD

YOUR GUIDE TO FINANCIAL CLARITY

Growing up, my dad was a firm believer in structure. You could find him saying, "kids need structure," to anyone who would listen. In fact, there was a song at night he would chant: "wash your face, brush your teeth, go to bed." He isn't alone, either, in valuing structure. Successful athletes and leaders credit their structure and routines to their success both professionally and personally. When I started working with clients, I also wanted to build a framework that I could use consistently in any situation that would give them the best chance of success with their financial decision-making not just when they were with me, but a skill they could learn and use throughout their life.

WHERE IT ALL BEGAN

Your relationship with money is one that will be with you until the day you die and even afterwards (hello, estate planning!). It is a skill, a hobby, a relationship all tied into one that needs time, love, and patience as there will be mistakes made along the way. You have picked up this book for a reason. Let's pause here for you to note what that reason is. This will help serve as a reminder as you go through the book and see how far you have come on growing your relationship with money.

PROMPTS

Your Personal Why?

_____.

My reason why I am reading this book is

_____.

This book will be like peeking into people's homes to see how and what financial conversations might look like at various points in your life. As a kid—who am I kidding?—even now, I walk by homes wondering what do they do for work. How did they make their money? Who makes the financial decisions in the house? Are they in debt? Is it a home of love and laughter or fear and danger inside? I wrote this book as if we have pulled back the curtain and are a fly on the wall seeing how different people handle talking about money at different life stages.

The Money Mindset Method

THE ORIGIN

It is important to understand how and know where your money beliefs come from. I have broken it down into three main pillars.

Our background

Back to the conversation about peeking into people's homes . . . each home talks about money differently and usually only behind closed doors. Even kids growing up in the same home receive different messages depending on birth order, career stages of the adults, and relationship status (married, divorced, widow, etc.). At my home growing up, after we went to the mall we would hide the shopping bags from my dad. I guess now it is trying to hide the Amazon boxes from your family. The funny thing later in life, I realized, my dad paid the bills so I am not sure what we were hiding, but this was part of my background.

Religion/cultural

There are various types of references to money and depending on your religious environment and/or culture it can affect your financial beliefs as well. For example: "The love of money is the root of all evil" (1 Timothy 6:10). Tithing (donating 10% of income) reflects the importance of giving back to the community and supporting others. Wealth (Artha) is one of the four goals of life but should be pursued ethically and in balance with Dharma (righteousness). Islamic law makes it a man's duty to financially support his wife and children, even if his wife earns her own income, and 1 Timothy 5:8 shares, "Anyone who does not provide for their relatives . . . has denied the faith and is worse than an unbeliever." Religious and cultural teachings about money can lead to conflicts, guilt, or confusion when personal financial goals or modern lifestyles seem to contradict traditional values.

Experiences

Your experiences have a way of shaping how you see the world and your finances. The wins bring confidence and gratitude, while the challenges shape and build or take you down in unexpected ways. Ever had one bad experience make you skeptical about an entire group or industry? For instance—I've had a couple of frustrating run-ins with car mechanics taking advantage of my lack of knowledge, and now I find myself driving around with a warning light on longer than I'd like to admit. But here's the kicker: it's not the whole industry; it's about two bad experiences. Yet it is challenging to separate the two things when emotions are involved. Our experiences don't define everything—they just add layers to our story, shaping how we move forward.

You currently have your money mindset based on the three pillars outlined previously, and yet society has told you not to talk about money with others, not allowing you to grow your money mindset. Then, let me ask you, how are you supposed to improve, shift, or grow your money mindset without access to healthy conversations, practical tools, and resources?

Welcome to *Conversations with Your Financial Therapist*. I am glad you are here. I wanted to create a safe place for you to learn, explore, and grow your personal relationship with money.

THE FRAMEWORK

The Money Mindset Method, defined in this book, is the framework to help guide you through financial conversations that you can use for any type of financial decision with yourself, a partner, family members, or even your financial advisor.

The Money Mindset Method

MONEY is the acronym we will be using to define the framework. It is broken down into these five actions:

M = Make conversations comfortable
O = One by one
N = Nurture shared goals
E = Evaluate practical solutions
Y = Yes to compassion

M = Make conversations comfortable

Set the tone for open, honest money discussions.

Openness with yourself and others is an important part of the process of allowing yourself to be free from guilt and shame about money among other emotions that might show up when getting ready to have a financial conversation. Setting the environment to feel comfortable and safe helps to build trust and financial intimacy. This transparency and openness promotes healthier financial habits and stronger relationships over time, enabling you to make informed decisions and achieve your financial goals with yourself and others.

Environment can include location, temperature, noise level, time of day, and so on—and emotional state from outside stressors, food intake or lack of, and with whom the people are to have conversations. Take the time to set yourself up for success by planning ahead.

O = One by one

Don't overload the conversation. Tackle one money topic at a time.

Starting simple and staying focused in financial conversations is crucial because it's easy to complicate discussions or introduce multiple issues at once. To avoid this, do a brainstorm session and list all your questions. Then agree on one topic to focus on per meeting.

Ways to keep this task on track include setting a specific time limit for each person to talk after the brainstorm to avoid fatigue and using bullet points or outlines to help identify a theme.

Once you see a common theme, select that as your topic to focus on. Write it down. Keep it handy to reference throughout your meeting(s).

Tip: Create a unique code word for when the conversation gets too heated or frustration arises, allowing for necessary breaks without derailing progress. It is also important at this time of selecting the code word how and when you will come back to resume the conversation after the word is used. If possible, resuming the conversation the same day helps maintain momentum and resolve issues effectively. This approach promotes clarity, reduces stress, and fosters healthier financial communication knowing that you can pause the conversation, take a walk or dance break, and come back with a fresh perspective.

N = Nurture shared goals
Collaborate to align goals and build mutual trust for your financial future.

Finding common ground after identifying the issue is essential for smoother financial conversations. It helps keep the discussion focused by removing distractions with a united goal. Understanding each other's viewpoints will make it easier to agree on solutions and build trust. This shared understanding of why the shared goal is important to you both will help decrease the disagreements together and reduce conflict, making it easier to find solutions that work for both of you when you are working toward the shared goal.

E = Evaluate practical solutions
Find solutions that are actually realistic and actionable.

Once you've found a common goal it's time to look for practical solutions together. Focus on finding realistic answers that fit your financial limits and resources. Knowing your boundaries helps you make decisions that match your goals and align with your values. This will be the time to review your resources, ask the what-if questions, and possibly think outside the box for solutions.

Y = Yes to compassion

Be gentle with yourself and others—money is emotional, and that's okay!

Kindness and empathy are essential in most financial discussions. Everyone makes mistakes, and most money issues are fixable. Approaching these conversations with empathy helps us understand one another's challenges and find solutions together. Being kind to ourselves enables growth and learning from past experiences, while extending empathy builds trust and strengthens relationships. Together, these qualities create a supportive environment where we can navigate financial challenges with compassion and understanding.

The Money Mindset Method can and should be used for small and large financial decisions. The more practice you have working through each step, the easier it will be for when the larger financial discussions show up later in life. Just like with learning a new hobby, *practice makes progress*. Your relationship with money will always be shifting and changing. Having a tool you can use repeatedly with yourself, a partner, your kids, family members, or in your career can help reduce the stress, uncertainty, and awkwardness, while increasing your health and wealth.

WHAT FINANCIAL LESSONS DID YOU LEARN FROM YOUR PARENTS?

SOURCE: LET'S TALK FINANCES CONVERSATION CARDS

CHAPTER TWO

WELCOME TO ADULTHOOD

WHERE FINANCIAL FREEDOM MEETS CONFUSION

> *This chapter features Gabe, Madison, and Sophia.*
>
> *Gabe is 22 years old and is about to graduate from college and move to New York City. He is unsure of where to live, what it will cost, or how long he can stay on the family cell phone plan. He has been living with support from his parents up until now and feels lost about what to do next. Becoming an adult feels overwhelming.*
>
> *Madison is working at the diner in town, age 19, and really proud to be out on her own. Even if it doesn't look glamorous to others, it is much better than her childhood home life. She relies on Cannonball, her beloved car, to get to and from work until one day, she can't.*
>
> *Sophia is over the crazy life of living half in college life mode and half in the real world. At the age of 24, she is living with several roommates, has a full-time job, and is paying off her student loans. She wants to be both independent and financially responsible. Sophia's anxiety is kicking into overdrive leaving her paralyzed to make any decisions, afraid she will make the wrong one. The struggle is real for her.*
>
> *Script 1: Make the Damn Call!*
>
> *Script 2: Don't Let Your Mind Be the Weakness Muscle*

You know *everything*, and yet nothing. Being a young adult, at least for me, felt freeing, empowering, and confusing. It doesn't seem I am alone in all of these feelings.

We spend most of our teen years trying to be an adult, yet when it is time, we are thrown out into the world with little real-life guidance. Especially when it comes to how to make smart financial decisions like how to buy a car, how much to spend on housing, even where to grocery shop and how much we can spend on food each week. Who knew all these decisions could add up to a lot of money, potential debt, and stress in our lives in our late teens and early twenties?

Welcome to Adulthood

Our education system does not do a good job at teaching us how to be financially responsible adults. I see this with clients with high school educations all the way to high-powered ivy-educated doctors and lawyers. It doesn't matter how many years you spend in school, knowing the value of a dollar and the emotional toll of spending and saving are not discussed. Which leaves you as an adult not set up for success.

LEARNING ABOUT MONEY 101

Gabe

Gabe seems to have it all and nothing at the same time. He is just about to graduate top of his class, move to the big city with a high-paying consulting job, yet he has no idea what that all really means. Gabe grew up in a household where his job was to get good grades and his parent's role was to pay for his needs, wants, and lifestyle. He has had a loving family, warm meals, and a stable childhood. While this might seem dreamy to most, what happens now when Gabe steps out into the real world without ever knowing the value of a dollar, how to pay a bill, or manage his paycheck each month?

The general definition of the value of a dollar is defined as understanding the worth of money, particularly through hard work, responsible spending, and financial awareness.

Moments in our growing up revealed how our families treated and respected money and those shaped us on what the value of a dollar means. Each person has a unique view on the value of money. For example, let's take a summer vacation for a family of four. For one family it involves a plane ticket, fancy hotels, and museums for $10,000 for a week; for others it is driving, camping, and rock climbing for a week for $1,000. Both vacations will lead to core memories for the families, yet the one family values sleeping in air conditioning more than another. The point is we each value money differently and that is shown in how and where we spend it. That is true for people with and without money.

When you come from nothing, the value of the dollar is abstract. Whether it is time to go back to school, buy new clothes, or sign up for a class field trip, money is just a fantasy. Yet, when you have wealth, the value of a dollar is also abstract, as your bills are all paid for and cars appear when you turn 16 without a worry.

The question then is, how do you learn the value of money?

Usually it starts in the young adult era, the time when you are paying for bills on your own, paying taxes, and rent. Often comes with an "oh, shit" feeling after several paychecks come in and out and yet you have no idea where the money went.

PROMPTS

I learned the value of money from _____.

I value the _____ that money provides for me.

CREDIT CARDS AND CHAOS

Madison

Madison's car broke down on the way from home to work in the early morning hours with no one around. No surprise to her as her car was an old clunker she'd named *Cannonball*. She saved every penny for months to buy her beloved Cannonball to help her get to work and back, but now it needed a new timing belt and two new tires at the price of $627! Madison had only $33 dollars in her checking account. So when the salesman offered her a credit card and 20% savings, she jumped at the chance without reading the fine print or understanding how or when to pay it off. The $627 bill at a 24% interest rate in the end will cost her a lot more in actual money and comes with the emotional stress when the bill arrives every month. Madison knew she didn't have the money to pay it off in the coming months, yet she felt she had no other option for her car to keep running.

Madison isn't alone. This recently happened to me when I noticed I had a nail in a tire and I dropped by a local tire shop to get a patch. The next thing I knew the mechanic told me I needed four new tires, shared with me an invoice for over $1,000, and told me, "Not to worry, I can open a credit card and get you a discount plus free tire rotation." Like he was doing *me* a favor. My gut told me this didn't feel or look right. I am not a tire expert, but I knew to get a second opinion—which I did. Guess what? All it needed was a patch for $35. The tires still had over 10,000 miles left on them. I have to say I didn't feel good walking out of the first store. I felt pissed off, wanted to cry for feeling dumb about cars and confused about what I was supposed to do. Thankfully I called a few friends who know about cars, asked some simple questions, and found a shop that I could trust. Otherwise this would have been a large expense I was not expecting, like Madison.

Getting a credit card is just a click away. You are asked to open a card everywhere these days, from checking out at a retail store to flying on an airplane. Society makes it easy to get, yet does little to educate the end user on the impact of use, especially if you take on credit card debt early on in life. Mismanaged credit card use in your youth can play a role in your life moving forward with additional interest payments (aka more money to the bank than in your pocket), a poor credit score, and financial stress.

A few years back, my five-year-old daughter saw that I was tapping the credit card to pay for the week's groceries and asked, "How much is on that thing?" Great question, little one. The financial value on each credit card depends on the person's credit limit. But how do I have that conversation with a five-year-old? It made me think about when I used to go to the store with my dad. When we would get to the checkout counter, he would take out the dollar bills and coins from his pocket, jiggle around the change, and

CONVERSATIONS WITH YOUR FINANCIAL THERAPIST

have me count out the amount to give to the cashier and figure out the change. To a kid, this was a big job and often I was excited to count out the money. I was touching and seeing the dollars that were paying for our food that week. Yet now with a tap and digital transfer, how do we teach the younger generation about money? The result is most don't and instead learn on their own through trial and error.

We mandate that to drive a car you must pass a test to know the rules of the road, yet at 18 you are able to open a credit card up with zero knowledge of how to use it, which can be dangerous to many people. It's like giving the keys of a complex tower crane that should only be used by skilled professionals to someone off the street with no training. For most it would lead to disaster. The same is true with credit cards.

> ## PROMPTS
>
> What do you recall about getting your first credit card?
>
> ___
>
> Has it helped or hindered you in life?
>
> ___

The average credit card debt for Gen Z is $9,592.[1] At the average APR (annual percentage rate) of 24% and paying the minimum amount, it will take over **nine years** to pay that back. Let me say that again: nine years of paying the minimum payment amount to be debt free if you don't add any additional debt in those years. You will also pay over $13,000 in interest (that is what you are paying the bank to borrow the money). The $9,592 of debt over nine years will cost you over $22,000.

I tell my clients to wave at the bank building when they see it as they are paying for the lights to be on with every interest payment they make. I don't know about you, but I would rather that money go toward my electric bill.

Welcome to Adulthood

Here's the average debt balances by age group:

- Gex Z (ages 18–23): $9,593
- Millennials (ages 24–39): $78,396
- Gen X (ages 40–55): $135,841
- Baby boomers (ages 56–74): $96,984
- Silent generation (ages 75 and above): $40,925[2]

Where are you with these averages? Above or below?

Madison believed she was doing the right thing by paying the $25 a month minimum payment since that is what the bank statement said. She didn't realize that the $627 for tires and repairs would lead to paying the bank an extra $252.12 in interest (24%) and three years to pay it off.[3] Yikes.

THE BALANCING ACT OF EDUCATION AND STUDENT LOANS

Sophia

Sophia is a vibrant 24-year-old recent college graduate in graphic design ready to take on the world in her first real job. She left college not just with a degree but also with $18,000 in student loans.

This is a very exciting time for Sophia, with a lot of new adventures and unknowns ahead of her; one big adventure is finances. After living with four roommates in college, she wants to live alone in a studio apartment to avoid dealing with messy roommates and loud late nights. In theory this sounds like a great next move for her, but how can she afford to live alone and make timely payments for rent, living expenses, and student loans?

During her college years, student loan debt seemed normal, heck every other person around her had it. Yet it was not discussed how, when, and where to pay it off the quickest. Soon after graduation, Sophia's sleepless nights start and the feeling of anxiety of owing more than she can pay back settled in.

This is a familiar situation for a lot of young adults, which often leads people to throw their hands up and say, "I will never win here," and accumulate more debt.

In fact, one out of every two people that graduates college carries a student loan with an average amount of $29,400.[4] Just as with credit cards, they often don't realize that the roughly $30,000 that pays for school is also borrowed money at an interest rate, which means they will end up paying more than the amount borrowed. Then add in starting salaries (which are generally low) for young professionals, the rising cost of housing, and inflation, well ... you get it. Paying off student loans comes at a much higher cost than they might have been aware of when signing on the dotted line.

PROMPTS

I wish I knew _____ about student loans.

Paying off my student loans means _____ to me.

With our three young adults, Gabe, Madison, and Sophia, at the cusp of making money decisions and learning about how to work with debt, using the Money Mindset Method will guide them through the decision-making process.

M = Make conversations comfortable

O = One by one

N = Nurture shared goals

E = Evaluate practical solutions

Y = Yes to compassion

Just because you are flying solo does not give you permission to skip any of the steps. Treat yourself like you would an important client.

Welcome to Adulthood

Schedule a meeting with yourself to have these conversations. It is an important step in setting your intentions and creating realistic goals. Find a time and place that enables you to be comfortable, including the temperature of the room, the noise level, and scents around you.

Here is what it looked like for our friends:

Gabe	Madison	Sophia
Craves structure and a good plan. He blocks the time in his calendar so he can sit down and focus on his goal without interruptions. Thursday morning from 8 to 9 a.m. he's at the kitchen table with a coffee and notebook after his workout and before he dives into studying for finals. He also sets a timer to let him know when to stop as he doesn't want to be late for the library and doesn't also want to keep checking the clock.	Feels best when she is out in nature. On her Thursday hike this week, she decided to take a journal, her credit card statement, and a pen. She gives herself time to walk and think, then pause and write, and then walk and think again. Being outside helps her regulate her nervous system, which goes into overdrive when dealing with money.	For Sophia, since she is currently living with several roommates, her house is not the right place for this. She selects her favorite coffee shop on a Sunday morning to sit down with her computer to use as a journal to start the process of having some real conversations with herself about her living situation, adulting, and more.

M = Make conversations comfortable

O = One by one

N = Nurture shared goals

E = Evaluate practical solutions

Y = Yes to compassion

Oftentimes with money conversations we get overwhelmed with all the details. This is a good point to stop, breathe, and check in with your body. In fact, take three deep breaths right now, then scan your body on where and how the emotions are showing up before you start to ask the questions to yourself. Place your hands on the area that you sense emotion,

CONVERSATIONS WITH YOUR FINANCIAL THERAPIST

this can be your lungs, stomach, head, back, and so on. By acknowledging the emotion, you are able to sit with it, validate it, and hopefully release it. As you go through this process at any time, stop and repeat this exercise.

Gabe	Madison	Sophia
Opens up his laptop, creates a new note: NYC PLAN. Sets a timer for 30 minutes to stay on task and not get distracted by looking at the clock.	Keeps putting off sitting down with herself to have the conversation as she is afraid of what she is going to find out. Finally, gathers the courage, stops hiking, opens up the latest credit card statement, and creates a goal in her journal.	Grabs a napkin at the coffee shop and writes on the back of it the one question she was going to stick to during her one-hour session today, focusing on figuring out whether she can live on her own.
I have no idea how to be an adult. I would rather stay at school.	I don't like the feeling about being in debt. How much in debt am I really?	I hate hearing the door slam every night at 3 a.m.! I can never go back to sleep and am grumpy all day. How can I get a solid night's sleep?
Where do I start? I have no idea how much it takes to live in New York City, and I never paid a bill before.	Holidays are coming and it's too easy to put more items on the cards and I don't want more debt.	If I live alone, will I be scared someone will break in? I'll have to sleep with the lights on.
I'm screwed. I can't do this. Will I be kicked off the family cell phone plan?	I hate owing anyone anything. Reminds me of being a kid and my mom owing my aunt $1,000 and it ruined their relationship for a while.	I don't want to be 40 years old and still paying off student loans. This debt is haunting me.
Common theme: Fear of the unknown is overwhelming, but not taking action is an action, too. I won't give up my dream job because of fear. I will figure out how to move and live on my own.	**Common theme:** Paying off the debt will give me the confidence that I can manage money "like a responsible adult."	**Common theme:** Physical safety and peace and quiet is important, so is financial peace of mind. I need to find a way to balance both for long-term sanity.

28

Welcome to Adulthood

Note: Several times while sitting at the coffee shop Sophia had the urge to leave. After taking a few deep breaths, giving herself a small pep talk (you can do this!), and writing down the simple one question she was going to work on, she was then able to refocus and begin the work again. Rome wasn't built in a day and neither will be your financial muscles.

Tip: Write your common theme or one focus area down and put it on a sticky note in front of you to stay focused when engaging in financial conversations.

M = Make conversations comfortable

O = One by one

N = Nurture shared goals

E = Evaluate practical solutions

Y = Yes to compassion

Understanding what your goal is and why it is important to you is a step you cannot skip. This is what will hold yourself accountable to and drive you to reach your goal. Your brain may have a lot of messaging going on. When you are doing this exercise solo, use this time to explore, discover, and dig into why this goal is important to you.

Identify three to five messages that are keeping you awake at night or with worry.

Write them down.

1. _____

2. _____

CONVERSATIONS WITH YOUR FINANCIAL THERAPIST

3. _____

4. _____

5. _____

What is the common theme showing up? _____

Therefore, this goal is important and unique to *you* because

_____

_____

_____

Here is a peek into what Gabe, Madison, and Sophia wrote down.

Gabe	Madison	Sophia
1. I have no idea where to start. 2. I am not going to know my way to work. I'll get lost. 3. Getting a consulting job has been my goal for the past few years; this is exciting. 4. What if I hate my job? 5. Will I have any friends?	1. I can't sleep at night because I am worried about money. 2. What is going to happen to my credit score when I need a new car? 3. Why can I never get ahead? 4. I don't want to be like my mom with money.	1. The door. The damn door. Hearing the door open and close all night long is driving me crazy, I can't get a good night sleep and when I don't sleep I am grumpy at work and at home. 2. Ugh, student loan debt will be with me forever. I just wish I had a magic wand for it to go away. 3. Living alone sounds amazing, but what if I fall and no one comes to find me for days?
Goal: To crush it in my new consulting job, feel good about the work, make some friends, and actually enjoy the new place I'm living in without forgetting to pay the bills.	**Goal:** To stop stressing about money and feel in control.	**Goal:** Figuring out how to actually feel like an adult without losing my mind.

Welcome to Adulthood

For example, Gabe's why is to make his parents proud. After spending so much time, money, and energy on his education he doesn't want to embarrass them by making a mistake. He wants to show them that he can and is ready to be an adult.

M = Make conversations comfortable

O = One by one

N = Nurture shared goals

E = Evaluate practical solutions

Y = Yes to compassion

Focus on finding realistic and effective solutions while being mindful of your financial limits. Understanding your boundaries helps in making sound financial decisions. You may not or, let's be more realistic at this stage of life, you probably do not know all your options available. Use this step to brainstorm, research, ask questions to people you know and people you don't. Some ideas might jump out at you and others might need a nudge from someone who has been where you were in the past. Learning how to talk about money and ask questions will be a helpful skill to grow and help you in the future.

Tip: Set a timer for 20 minutes and do a structured brainstorm to create options and possible opportunities to research.

Here is what our trio came up with:

Gabe	Madison	Sophia
I need to live close to work as I'll be working 70 hours a week. Google's rental apartments in the zip code. Ouch!	Take on extra shifts at the diner. Whatever I earn in that shift will go directly to the debt.	I gotta get out of my living situation, but I can never live alone.

CONVERSATIONS WITH YOUR FINANCIAL THERAPIST

Gabe	Madison	Sophia
Living alone won't be possible especially since I won't be home much; I need to look for a roommate. Let me ask around my friends if they know anyone looking for a roommate.	Put up fliers for babysitting (increase income during off hours).	I am paying $1,600 a month now. Where can I find a studio for that rent? Let me look online and call Jain. He recently moved out; maybe I can see who helped him.
I don't need a car. I need to sell that. I need to ask my dad how to do that. I don't know where to start. Work is going to be paying for my cell phone (phew).	Call the credit card company and ask for a reduction in APR rate. (See Script 1: Make the Damn Call!)	Is $1,400 a real number for me? If I am paying for all the bills myself? I need to review my pay-check and see.
Buying furniture? A bed? How the heck do you do that? ... Hmmmm ... I'm better off looking for a furnished apartment. Maybe the HR [human resources] department at work can help.		Can I ask for a raise or add freelance work? Am I willing to cook more and do less delivery to save money for my sanity?

PROMPTS

By not looking for a solution _____ will happen.

M = Make conversations comfortable

O = One by one

N = Nurture shared goals

E = Evaluate practical solutions

Y = Yes to compassion

A lot of emotions have probably come and gone while you are working through the Money Mindset Method. This last step is one not to miss. Our emotions are like waves; they will come and go, and so will your

Welcome to Adulthood

frustrations and wins with your relationship with money, so be kind to yourself and practice empathy.

While youth is on your side, experience isn't yet. The human brain's frontal lobe, especially the prefrontal cortex, isn't fully mature until about the age of 25. You will make mistakes along your journey. When you do, acknowledge it, laugh at them, and learn from it. It won't be your last time you will have to adjust your financial goals, so be kind to yourself.

Once more, let's turn the page to see how Gabe, Madison, and Sophia handle something that "should" be easy, but often we find difficult—practicing kindness to ourselves.

Gabe	Madison	Sophia
I appreciate everything my parents have done for me to get me to where I am today.	Say sorry to myself. You did what you needed to do in that situation and have come up with a plan to pay off the debt.	As much as I want to live alone, I might need to adjust to living with one or two roommates versus four right now.
I need to take ownership now in my future.	Learn that it is important to have a car fund or emergency fund for moments like this.	It is okay if I am not able to do it all today. I am moving forward.
I am going to mess this up and it will be okay. I am only human as long as I don't ignore the mistakes I can fix them. (See Script 2: Don't Let Your Mind Be the Weakness Muscle.)	Create a grateful practice at red lights that you are driving a safe car to help you live the beautiful life you have.	I am proud of where I am going.

Where Are They Now?

Gabe struggled with not having all the answers right away. Moving, figuring out sheet sizes for his new bed, and how many cups to buy, along with where to live was very difficult for him and he didn't know on whom to lean. He wanted to be seen as an adult to his parents, HR leaders, and friends, yet silently he was struggling. After he went through the Money Mindset Method steps he realized that he did have options.

Gabe came up with three options.

1. His old roommate had a friend who was looking for a roommate 20 minutes from the office. He was a messy guy, but it was a place to live with little effort.
2. The HR manager suggested temporary housing just steps from the office that is fully furnished. Several new hires stayed in for the first 60 days to learn the area and demands of the job.
3. Just let his mom figure it all out. She loves a good project.

What Would You Do?

Gabe went with option 2. He moved into temporary housing for 60 days. During this time he realized he liked being steps away from the office to not wake up any earlier than he needed. At work he asked around to some of the junior consultants and found a furnished apartment of an employee who was on assignment for a year. This would give him a year to learn and grow with his finances and when he is ready again to decide what's next he will use the Money Mindset Method to explore the next phase.

PS: His dad was happy to see him come off the family cell phone plan :).

Where Are They Now?

Madison is celebrating the holidays in style this year. She is curled up on her boyfriend's couch smiling. Life has taken a sweet turn for her. While going through the Money Mindset Method she uncovered three options to get her to where she is today: out of credit card debt.

Welcome to Adulthood

1. If she wanted to pay off her debt by the holidays, she needed to work an additional 10 hours a month at the coffee shop. That would make for long days, but doable.
2. Her evenings were open, she could find a babysitting job twice a week, which would cut into her social life, but then again what social life?
3. Call the credit card company and ask to reduce the interest rate from 24% to 18%, which will help with the repayment, and increase her payments to $100/month, which will reduce the interest amount and have it paid off in seven months.

What Would You Do?

Madison did a combination of all of these. She first called the credit card company (See Script 1: Make the Damn Call!) and received a temporary reduction to 18% for six months; this gave her the push to get it paid off in this time frame. She created a "get out of debt" jar at home to keep the additional funds. One of her regular customers became a Saturday night babysitting client, and she picked up extra shifts at the coffee shop. In fact, one of those shifts is when she met José, her new boyfriend.

Where Are They Now?

Sophia realized that her well-being is a priority. For her, well-being means a quieter living environment and money to put toward her student loans. The stress of constantly being annoyed at her roommates and financial pressures were affecting her health, relationships with friends, and sleep.

Sophia came up with three options:

1. A studio apartment an hour from work that was in a four-story walk up and was so tiny she could brush her teeth, shower, and use the toilet all at the same time, but it would be all her own.
2. She walked past an apartment for rent in her neighborhood. It would be for two people, which will help her split the bills and stay in the area of her friends. Now, which friend to move in with?
3. Move home, save money, pay off her student loans as quickly as possible, and find a remote job to enable her to do this.

What Would You Do?

Sophia decided to go with option 2. That way she can balance paying her bills and reduce the noise of so many roommates. It happens that one of her current roommates was also unhappy with their current living situation. After a few months in their new apartment, they worked out a nice routine, started cooking dinners together (and washing the dishes), which enabled Sophia to start paying off her student loan payments on time and increased her health.

Welcome to Adulthood

MONEY MANTRA

I am wealthy, focused, and empowered.
I am and have enough.
I trust my decisions and honor my growth.
Every step I take builds freedom, abundance, and peace.

XOXO, Your Future Self

DO YOU BELIEVE YOU ARE WORTHY OF THE MONEY YOU EARN?

WHY OR WHY NOT?

SOURCE: LET'S TALK FINANCES CONVERSATION CARDS

CHAPTER THREE

FROM BURNOUT TO BREAKTHROUGH

TAKING CHARGE OF YOUR CAREER

CONVERSATIONS WITH YOUR FINANCIAL THERAPIST

This chapter features Gabe and Averi.

Gabe has been at his job for three years and is performing well. He is the first to get to work and usually the last to leave, about 1 a.m. on some nights. He is about to head into his review with his boss and feels pretty good about his performance.

Averi has been with the same law firm for 10 years and is starting to get the itch to go out on her own or switch firms. Change doesn't come easy for her and it all seems overwhelming, yet she knows it is needed for a better life–work balance and salary. She has noticed lately that she has been feeling tired and losing weight, which are signs her Crohn's could be flaring up. On a recent appointment, her doctor asked about her stress levels, which she laughed at knowing she has been overdoing it at the office and overlooking her health.

Script 3: Is It Time to Shift My Career? Advice Needed

Script 4: Leveling Up: A Conversation on Promotions in the Workplace

Your career is more than just a paycheck—it's a major player in how you view and manage money. Whether you're thriving in a job you love or navigating a tough work environment, your career shapes your earning potential, spending habits, and financial priorities. A fulfilling role can make money feel like a tool for your passions, while a stressful one might make it seem like a reward for sacrifices. Even career changes teach valuable lessons about resilience and adapting financially. By understanding this connection, you can align your career and finances to support the life you want to build.

PROMPTS

How did you feel when you earned your first paycheck? _____

Did you save or spend it? _____

What do you do now with your paychecks?_____

Your career isn't just about earning money; it also shapes how you feel about money and its role in your life. Depending on the job, the management, the scope of work, location, and so on, earning the same salary from one company to the next can feel different. Also, depending on your lifestyle the same $80,000 income can feel different. I was working with a couple a few years ago where after working for almost 20 years, he was a successful executive. The wife retired 10 years earlier since he was making double of what they both made when they first met, but now when they looked at their finances they were stressed. When they were young and each making $40,000, they were very conscious about their spending and saving and so were their friends. When they were starting out they went to dive bars, festivals, and friends' houses for dinners; today, they are members of a country club, dinners out are hundreds of dollars, and their mortgage is twice as much. All this has led to sleepless nights about not having enough in savings as they age. When we stepped back, lifestyle creep was at play here, expectations of what they thought an executive should look like took up his entire paycheck now. Meaning, just because you are earning more money does not mean you are saving more money. Lifestyle creep is real and something to keep in mind as you gain more success in your career and your income increases. This couple took the time to reassess their spending habits, which included a lower car payment and less impulsive shopping, and shifted the additional funds each month into savings. Taking the time to pause, reflect, and readjust was key to their financial future.

On your career journey there will be several times to pause and assess if how you are managing your finances is still working for you. It's important to do this. Am I happy with my job, the salary, and do I feel appreciated for my contributions?

Gabe

Gabe is at this point of self-reflection after three years with his company. He has learned a lot in the last few years, working hard daily, coming in early, working weekends, and receiving frequent praise from his boss. It is time for his annual review and Gabe walks in confident but leaves confused. He was right to feel good walking in, the boss had a lot of great feedback for him including that they are going to promote him to the next level next month. This role will include a larger scope of work, more client-facing opportunities, and management of the interns that summer. What was not clear was when the increase in salary would come. The boss left it vague for when the money will catch up with the promotion, which is not sitting well for Gabe. He is aware they recently lost a member of the team and that person's work was going to be absorbed by the current team, which to him means even longer hours and additional stress. He was failing to see the upside of the promotion. The messaging he received from management was that he should be excited that they valued him and see a strong future with him in management. They were unclear on when exactly they would increase his salary, but said sometime the next year.

This is called a *dry promotion*. We are seeing more and more of this in the workplace. Some reasons for this are that companies are tight on finances or merging two businesses with various people leaving or changing roles. The work still needs to get done, so management reallocates the workload to the remaining staff without a pay increase.

A dry promotion—when you take on new responsibilities without a corresponding increase in pay or benefits—can leave you feeling undervalued and frustrated. While it may initially feel like a recognition of your skills, the lack of tangible rewards often overshadows the accomplishment. This can lead to feelings of resentment, as the additional workload doesn't match the compensation or acknowledgment received. Over time, it may also cause burnout or disengagement, even resentment, as the imbalance between effort and reward takes its toll. Ultimately, a dry promotion can diminish motivation and trust,

From Burnout to Breakthrough

leaving you questioning your worth and long-term career goals, which is where Gabe is at. He is going to use the Money Mindset Method with his human resources (HR) partner to evaluate if the current salary he has with the current scope of work is right for him and if not, what his options are.

Averi

Averi is also kicking butt at work and has been moving up the ranks at her law firm over the past decade. She is seeing success in both her caseload and bank account, which both feel good. Yet her health has been declining. She is tired all the time, losing weight (and not in the good way), and finding herself going to the doctor's (and bathroom) more for management of her Crohn's disease. Recently several of her law school friends left their big firm to pursue smaller boutique firms or work for themselves, which has piqued Averi's interest. In corporate law, the average work week is 65–80 hours versus a smaller firm, which is 45–55 hours, and from what she is hearing the pay could be the same.

I've spoken with several HR leaders and they say that the best time to look for a new job is while you are employed and happy. By keeping yourself aware of what is out there, networking and understanding the market will help you for when you are ready to make the move. While keeping your options open, you should not inform your current employer you are looking for new employment. It is best to use personal devices in your search, avoid work time for job hunting, and keep it off your colleagues' radar. Networking discreetly, through LinkedIn or industry events, can help uncover leads without making your intentions obvious. Schedule interviews during nonwork hours or use personal leave, and maintain strong performance in your current role to protect your reputation.

Ready. Set. Go.

Define your goals of what you are looking for if you were to leave, whether it's higher pay, career growth, or better work–life balance, and tailor your applications to match each opportunity. This will help guide the conversations with potential new employers to see if they are the right match for where you are today with your personal goals and desires. When offers come in, compare them thoughtfully to ensure they align with your personal and professional goals.

Let's pull back the curtains at Gabe's apartment and Averi's home to see how they use the Money Mindset Method to explore their next career moves.

M = Make conversations comfortable

O = One by one

N = Nurture shared goals

E = Evaluate practical solutions

Y = Yes to compassion

Having a conversation with someone you are not too familiar with, such as a boss or HR partner, may be a challenge as you don't necessarily know what will make them comfortable. Think about a time when you did have a successful conversation with them. What time of day was it? What day of the week was it? What part of the fiscal cycle was it? All of these can factor on the outcome of the conversation.

You might also be unsure of whom to have a professional conversation with as it might not be something you do often. Talking about your career goals and financial expectations can be a very vulnerable experience for most people. I know for me, at different phases of my life, I was able to reach out to different people. At one point it was my parents, then a mentor when I was in the corporate world, a romantic partner who believed in me, an old classmate who was starting a business, and at another point a group of friends I met at a coffee shop who became my board of directors, as I like to call them. Averi is having a dilemma now of whom to brainstorm with about whether or not she is ready to make a career change. After giving it some thought, she decided to reach out to an old classmate who made the career decision to start his own practice three years earlier. Henry was happy to hear from her when she called last week.

From Burnout to Breakthrough

Averi	Gabe
Considering leaving her current firm brings up a lot of emotions for Averi. Change isn't something she enjoys. For the most part, she has been happy, made friends, and feels valued. Yet, she is starting to have fatigue more often, and seeing her friends change roles she has a little envy as well. Henry has always been a straight shooter. He tells it like it is: the good, bad, and ugly. That is what she needs to hear to weigh the options of moving jobs. Averi just finished a big case, the week coming up is going to be light, so it's a good opportunity to not feel stressed about leaving work before 7 p.m. Averi and Henry agree to meet at 5 p.m. at an old favorite restaurant they used to go to in law school. (See Script 3: Is It Time to Shift My Career? Advice Needed.)	The promotion conversation Gabe had with his boss stated that if he had any questions on the promotion or salary increase to work with the HR partner for their organization. Gabe recalls meeting with the HR partner last year and having a good rapport. She mentioned she works from the office on Tuesdays and Thursdays and leaves by 4 p.m. to get her kids from school. Gabe sends her an email to meet in person the following week on a Tuesday morning at 10 a.m. This will allow him to have the conversation in person, which he prefers, and not have her rushed to walk out the door. (See Script 4: Leveling Up: A Conversation on Promotions in the Workplace.)

M = Make conversations comfortable

O = One by one

N = Nurture shared goals

E = Evaluate practical solutions

Y = Yes to compassion

Brainstorming time!

What are the questions, concerns, unknowns that you have regarding this career move? Now is the time to list them out, write them down, type them up, and find a common theme that is worrying you right now.

CONVERSATIONS WITH YOUR FINANCIAL THERAPIST

Overwhelmed with a lot of questions, Averi knows she needs to prepare for the meeting the same way she does for a case. She needs to pull out the facts, the unknowns, and identify who can answer them.

Averi	Gabe
• If I am not with a big firm, will people take me seriously as an attorney? • Will I lose the networking opportunities I have now? • How do I know how much to charge? • What does it really cost to start a law firm? • What if I fail? • Is it really fewer hours of work? • What if nobody hires me?	• What will be my new measurements for success in this new role? • Will my manager change? • How much is the new salary increase, once it comes? • Will I receive management training to manage the interns? • When will the salary increase show up in my paycheck and will it be backdated? • What happens if the raise does not happen by *x* date?
Common theme: To understand the costs associated with running a new firm, including marketing and networking, which reaffirms self-doubt.	**Common theme:** To understand the expectations of the new job, and benefits of a new role including the salary increase timeline.

M = Make conversations comfortable

O = One by one

N = Nurture shared goals

E = Evaluate practical solutions

Y = Yes to compassion

The company has a goal and you have a personal goal (See Script 4: Leveling Up: A Conversation on Promotions in the Workplace.) Here is the opportunity to find the place where they could possibly overlap, allowing both the business and you to succeed.

From Burnout to Breakthrough

Averi	Gabe
Averi's goal in her career is to be well respected in her field of law. She wants to be paid appropriately, which is about $250,000/year plus a bonus. She wants to work less than 60 hours a week. She wants to get back to playing basket-ball on a team, which means leaving work before 8 p.m. during the week and increasing her networking/social life. She wants to feel better, be less stressed, and focus more on her health.	Gabe's goal is to grow his skills, including becoming a manager, to one day becoming an executive in the business. His goal is to also feel respected in his position. Also, He doesn't want to get burned out like he sees happening to so many of his older colleagues after years in business consulting. He wants to feel financially successful by earning a good salary without sacrificing his health, relationships, or happiness by overworking. Find the right balance.
	The company's goal is to grow their revenue. They want to increase the responsibility of the younger talent at lower pay to offset costs and increase skills of younger leaders. They are currently merging two compa-nies and trying to find redundant roles.
Shared goal: For Averi to build a successful and respected legal career that balances high earnings with a manageable workload, allowing time for personal fulfillment and social engagement.	**Shared goal:** To help Gabe grow as a leader and earn more, while the company boosts revenue and keeps costs down.

M = Make conversations comfortable

O = One by one

N = Nurture shared goals

E = Evaluate practical solutions

Y = Yes to compassion

CONVERSATIONS WITH YOUR FINANCIAL THERAPIST

To evaluate practical solutions in an HR conversation, focus on creating a balanced approach that addresses both the employee's concerns and the organization's objectives. Start by clearly identifying the issue and understanding the employee's perspective, including their goals, challenges, and needs. As the employee comes prepared to express their ideas, goals, and struggles within the current work environment, collaboratively explore potential solutions, such as offering skill development opportunities, adjusting responsibilities, or providing resources to improve work–life balance. Evaluate the feasibility of these options by considering budget, team dynamics, and organizational goals. Both sides can use open-ended questions to encourage dialogue and agree on measurable outcomes and follow-up steps. The key is to maintain transparency, fairness, and alignment with company policies while fostering a supportive environment for the employee.

Averi	Gabe
As they sit over dinner, Henry and Averi discuss practical solutions. They vary based on three situations: **Staying at a large firm:** Continue down the partner path, working 60–80 hours a week and creating boundaries for herself to leave work on days she has volleyball games. In addition, ask for a career mentor outside the firm, and join two new networking groups that will enable her to expand her reputation in the community.	Gabe walks into the conversation looking for answers on the salary increase. That is his main concern. He is nervous going in, but also knows if he doesn't have the conversation, resentment will build. The HR partner starts her day frustrated. The employee she met with before Gabe was called in for misconduct. Before Gabe walks in, she takes a deep breath and tries to refocus. She knows Gabe is performing well and is a talent the company wants to keep. Together they use the time to brainstorm options on how each can leave the meeting feeling it is a success. (See Script 4: Leveling Up: A Conversation on Promotions in the Workplace.)

From Burnout to Breakthrough

Averi	Gabe
Move to a boutique firm: The firm structure is already set up, the identity of the firm is established, the community is aware of the business. You are also walking into something established, with coworkers, rules, and expectations on what you will deliver to the firm. The firm's policies in the area are generally three days in the office and two days virtual, which will help with work–life balance. And the firm she is looking at has a pro bono side of the business that makes her smile. Henry hints at having her join his firm. As he shares with her, his practice is growing, his salary has doubled since leaving his old firm, and he is ready to talk about adding an associate.	His HR partner suggests that Gabe's increase will come after he shows a good performance for the new scope of work, which will likely come in the next review period next year.
Start her own firm: This is exciting and scary for her to even bring up. Henry outlines the start-up costs of opening a law firm, hiring staff, and finding new business. In the past three years, he has seen the reward of opening up his practice, but the first two years were financially very difficult for him. She listens closely and makes notes on his lessons learned along with the benefits of being the boss, which she will turn into a pro–con list.	HR is able to offer him an extra week of paid vacation, which is of value to him to help with avoiding burnout.
	HR also offers to pay for a new certification that will build his skill set (whether he stays or not).
	While Gabe is not thrilled with leaving the meeting without a salary increase, he feels valued by the additional time off and training. The HR partner feels good as well, leaving the meeting feeling they reached a solution that will retain top talent.

CONVERSATIONS WITH YOUR FINANCIAL THERAPIST

M = Make conversations comfortable

O = One by one

N = Nurture shared goals

E = Evaluate practical solutions

Y = Yes to compassion

Saying yes to compassion means recognizing that everyone—yourself, the company, and HR—is navigating challenges with the best intentions. Give yourself grace to voice concerns, trust that the company is balancing growth with employee well-being, and acknowledge HR's role in fostering fairness. Compassion creates space for understanding, leading to more productive and supportive solutions for all.

Averi	Gabe
Averi knows she is not going to make a quick move, but she also knows that if she doesn't evaluate her options, she will never know what is out there.	Ask questions; don't assume. Instead of assuming the raise would just come, creating and setting up a meeting allows Gabe to have a voice in the process.
She gives herself the time to sit with her feelings by taking bike rides and letting herself ponder life for the next few weeks.	Understanding that the business is also trying to succeed is having compassion for the managers and leaders in the business.
She reminds herself it is okay to set boundaries, take breaks, and pursue personal passions like volleyball without guilt.	Let go of frustrations—once the new agreements are in place, it is time to let go and enjoy the new role.

Where Are They Now?

Averi is chatting away at a networking event in town when she runs into a friend from her basketball team. They are sharing stories about their recent court cases, introducing each other to new friends in the room, and enjoying the night.

From Burnout to Breakthrough

Over the year, Averi came up with three options:

1. Stay with her law firm and ask them to sponsor the volleyball team.
2. Join Henry's firm and work 45 hours a week, enjoy the perks of working from home two days a week, and make more money than she did the prior year.
3. Start her own law firm—she is ready to take on the world. If Henry can do it, so can she.

What Would You Do?

After a few months of pondering her options, talking to a few more friends/mentors, Henry approached Averi with an offer she couldn't refuse. He provided her a path to partnership with him over the next five years. In addition, she could be responsible for the pro bono cases that give back to the community. The new job would give her flexibility with her time, case selection, and increase her finances. Option 2 was the winner for her.

Where Are They Now?

In the year since his promotion, Gabe has excelled in working with clients, managing the new interns, and with the extra week vacation he went to California to surf. He came up with three options:

1. Walk into his annual review with expectations of a raise, since it was promised a year ago.
2. Four months earlier he had a check-in meeting with his HR partner to ensure he was on track for the salary increase, leaving him feeling good about today's meeting.
3. Plans to hand over his resignation letter to a job offering as he doesn't feel valued in his current role.

CONVERSATIONS WITH YOUR FINANCIAL THERAPIST

What Would You Do?

Gabe is sitting at his desk thinking back to the conversation he had with the HR partner about the dry promotion he received with mixed emotions. He recalls that together they worked up a plan and four months ago when the annual salary conversations for increases were started, he set up a touch-base meeting to ensure his name was on the list. Management appreciated his proactive approach and reassured him that the raise was coming, and it ended up being a little more than he had hoped for.

From Burnout to Breakthrough

MONEY MANTRA

I am wealthy, focused, and empowered.

I am and have enough.

I trust my decisions and honor my growth.

Every step I take builds freedom, abundance, and peace.

XOXO, Your Future Self

HOW DID YOUR FAMILY DISCUSS MONEY, IF AT ALL?

**HOW WOULD YOU CHANGE
OR
HOW HAVE YOU CHANGED
THAT IN YOUR OWN
FAMILY?**

SOURCE: LET'S TALK FINANCES CONVERSATION CARDS

CHAPTER FOUR

MERGING MONEY AND MINDSETS WITH A LOVER

I love you, but . . . I'm not ready to share my finances with you.

CONVERSATIONS WITH YOUR FINANCIAL THERAPIST

> *This chapter features Madison and José, Averi and Sam, and also Sophia, who has married William since we last met her in Chapter 2.*
>
> *Madison, 20, and José, 21, are ready to move to the next stage of their relationship and have the official talk about money. They have been together for over a year, newly pregnant, and in need of planning for their future together as a family.*
>
> *Averi, 30, and Sam, 35, met nine months ago and while to some that might not sound that long, for them it felt like forever. They had both dated before, had serious relationships, and knew from day one of meeting that this was what a healthy relationship felt like to them.*
>
> *Script 5: The Codeword Is _____*
>
> *Script 6: Blending Family, Finances, and Food Bills*

Money is the second leading cause of relationships breaking up after infidelity. That can occur if you fall emotionally for someone without understanding their financial values, beliefs, debts, and realistic goals. If you think back to your relationships, when did you say I love and when did you share your financial information (credit score, debt, salary)? I ask this question when I present around the world and the answers are always the same no matter the size of the crowd, location, or age of the group. Hands will go up to share when they first said I love you, ranging from the first hour of meeting to about a year in, with the average being five months.

Next, I ask the question: when did you know about your partner's financial situation, their salary, credit score, debt, student loan status, and so on? Crickets. You can hear crickets or one person in the back will shout out "never!" They aren't alone in that answer either. As I open up the topic to the group, people start sharing and while the answers also vary from the first date (heard that once) to never, the average response is when they are talking about marriage or moving in together, which has been on average the nine-month mark.

So now you are emotionally madly in love with this person and just discovered key information that will shape your relationship in the future: from what kind of house you will live in and cars you will drive, to interest rates on loans and college planning for those one-day kids. One person's realistic goal could be another person's dream goal or not even on their radar. When you are not clear about your financial goals they become a dream, a dream that doesn't come true unless there is a plan. Now, plans can and will shift and change over time, but a dream stays a dream. A good way to start off on solid footing is early in the relationship start by setting realistic small goals for the week, the month, and feel the victory of the win together as a team. Slowly build to the larger financial goals now that you have the confidence of working together and understanding each other's financial mindset, habits, and obstacles. The earlier in the relationship you can start talking about money, the quicker you will create financial intimacy. Just like sexual intimacy it takes time, attention, creating a safe environment, a little bit of playfulness, and most of all builds a sense of trust and love with your partner.

Merging money can happen at various points in the journey of life, from dating (who pays for dinners versus nights out, etc.), to moving in together, to getting married, to having a child together, to caring for aging parents and dealing with siblings' disputes. It isn't just cut and dry when you get married out of love for one another that your financial values align. Communication is key to all aspects of a relationship including finances, yet it is a taboo topic for so many couples.

As I've mentioned, every person has a unique relationship with money based on three key areas: background, religion/cultural, and personal experiences with money. Now add in the layer that in most cultures people are taught to not talk about money with anyone around them. In fact 81% of people surveyed stated they were taught not to talk about money, but didn't know why,[1] creating a cycle of habits and patterns for generations. So what happens when you fall in love with someone, want to build a life

CONVERSATIONS WITH YOUR FINANCIAL THERAPIST

together, but haven't had a conversation about finances because you, like most of us, haven't seen healthy financial conversations take place? It can lead to a breakup based on miscommunication and misunderstandings.

By taking the time in the beginning of the relationship to understand your partner and their relationship with money it will help prevent future frustrations and misunderstandings. When you have an open and safe environment, it enables both people to revisit or share the overall health of their finances, including their credit score, debt, and/or any financial secrets. Like any hard conversation you try to avoid, the longer you leave it untold the more headspace it takes up with worry and anxiety when instead you could be working together on a solution.

Your relationship with money might also need to shift or take different shapes depending on where the journey takes you and your partner, especially when it comes to careers, job changes, moves, children, and other life events. Sometimes it may leave you with a sour taste, but hopefully more often with the taste of accomplishment.

Let's take a look at how Madison and José and Averi and Sam navigate these conversations.

Madison and José

Madison and José are like giddy teenagers in love. Ever since that chance meeting at the cafe several months ago the two have been inseparable. Madison's roommate is now including José in the monthly rent and bills as a housemate.

Recently at a family dinner at José's parents' house, the topic of getting married came up and while Madison was grinning ear to ear, her potential mother-in-law was not. José is the oldest son of three children. His parents had immigrated from Colombia and José was often looked at as the head of the family because he had been translating for his parents for years, from school report cards to calling the utility company. The thought of him marrying outside the Latin culture did not sit well with his parents as he was

Merging Money and Mindsets with a Lover

supposed to be the example for his siblings. When Madison wasn't feeling well a few weeks later and took a pregnancy test, everyone was surprised, including Madison and José. They were over the moon happy, ready to get married and start a family. They also knew they needed to sit down and have an adult conversation about money to figure out their options instead of just winging it as they were doing now.

* * *

Averi and Sam

Across town, sitting over a candlelight dinner, sharing childhood stories, dreams of the future, holding hands, and sipping wine, Averi and Sam knew this was what forever felt like. They had been dating just over nine months, were about to go on their first real vacation together (a week in California wine country), and dreaming of moving in together as they are already spending almost every night together.

Averi grew up with mixed messages about money beliefs. She had seen her parents fight over the smallest amounts of money. They had divorced when Averi was a young child and what to her just seemed like a haircut all of a sudden was a shouting match, leaving her feeling guilty for causing such trouble to people she loved. As she grew up and started to date, her money trauma showed up in small ways. She never wanted to feel that she was a reason for a fight or upset feelings especially when it came to money. Once she started making her own money, Averi found herself overpaying for things, picking up the bill for dinners with friends, and never being in debt to a friend for a vacation or a gift. This included the recent bachelorette party she went on. It annoyed her all weekend that the maid of honor just kept saying, "We will settle the bill next week." She felt lost and out of control not knowing how much she was spending all weekend and it gave her a stomachache knowing she would owe someone money next week. But now that she and Sam were talking about moving in together and combining finances, how could she "trouble" someone else with her student loan debt from law school? The feelings of being a financial burden that she first felt as a young child started to show up. Her gut reaction was to run away from Sam. But she was ready to face these issues head on using the Money Mindset Method with Sam to help both of them understand each other better and set them up for success.

Sam noticed that when she talked to Averi about moving into her house that Averi had a physical response to pull away just slightly. While at first she took it to be just new relationship jitters, as time went on she noticed it more and not just for the big conversations like moving in together but also for their upcoming trip to California. Sam had a job she loved, made some early real estate investments that have paid off, and was ready to start the next chapter of her life with a partner she could love forever.

Tip: If you need help with these conversations use the "Let's Talk About Finances Conversation Cards: Couple's Edition"[2] to guide you. Available on Amazon.

Financial intimacy: Being able to discuss money matters without judgment, fear, or hidden agendas.[3]

A GOAL WITHOUT A PLAN IS JUST A DREAM

Pillow talk in the beginning stages of a relationship often is a time to share dreams, hopes, plans for the future. When moving from the dreaming stage into real-life plans, it is important to understand why your partner is so passionate about making their goals a reality. For some it might be owning

Merging Money and Mindsets with a Lover

their own home one day because they grew up moving around frequently and always left with a feeling of uncertainty about the future. Or they are being frugal for three years so they can travel the world for a year to fulfill a lifelong dream at the age of 50. Or maybe paying for college for their kids is their number one goal as they were handed a mountain of student loans to start their life off and don't want to do that to the next generation. There are hundreds, thousands, of financial goals people may have, and usually more than one.

THE DIFFERENT SHAPES OF COMBINING MONEY

Combining money looks and feels different to each couple. There are a few common ways I see people do the math equations. Think of a lava lamp. The lamp creates similar yet different shapes. The same is true when two people are combining finances. It will take a shape, maybe one you are familiar with or looks slightly similar to how you were raised, although over time it can change shapes as life moves forward.

Taking the time to build your financial intimacy at any stage of your relationship is important. The earlier you embrace this topic, the healthier your financial life and financial decision-making will become over time.

For example, when it came to sharing bills, Madison wanted to pay the heating bill because it symbolized her keeping a warm home, which she didn't often have as a child. The higher thermostat temperature means a higher bill, and she was willing to pay that cost.

The goal here is to build understanding, shared values, and respect ... not resentment. Understanding the why will help identify how best to share the expenses, experiences, and investments of life's journey.

CONVERSATIONS WITH YOUR FINANCIAL THERAPIST

BUILD THE FOUNDATION TOGETHER AS KNOWLEDGE IS POWER

For any shape of combining money, here are three steps all couples can start with:

Map your money

- Create a joint list of financial activities (a financial Yes! Plan to spending)
- Note: A recommended guideline is 50% needs, 30% wants, 20% savings.

Oh shit! emergency fund

- Identify a realistic goal to have in this account and what it can be used for.
- Example: $5,000 in a high-yield savings account to be used for home emergencies or death-in-the-family type of emergencies.

The big picture

- List your assets and liabilities in one place to give a holistic view of your financial situation.
- Knowledge is power: 58% know their own net worth, and only 38% know their partner's.
- More people are familiar with Elon Musk's net worth (28%) than their own family's (24%).[4]

Next, take some time to see how you can do the following:

- Be bigger together.
- Look at ways to increase your net worth together.

62

- Buy more assets (save/invest more).
- Pay down debts (begin with high-interest loans or the smallest dollar amount).
- Maximize tax advantages (retirement accounts, file taxes jointly, etc.).
- Know the whos and the whats:
  - Establish roles for bill paying and banking system.

> **Tip:** Delegate a family CFO whose role is to establish meetings, ensure taxes are sent in, and annual meetings with advisors are made.

PICKING YOUR WAY TO MERGE MONEY IS A LITTLE LIKE CHOOSING YOUR LAVA LAMP COLORS

It is a personal preference.

Here are five options to choose from when merging money with a partner.

All-In

Only 43% of American couples currently have joint accounts.[5] Clients often share with me that they set up their money with the all-in method as this is what was done by their parents. This goes back to how we get our money beliefs based on our backgrounds. Our money mindset and habits are often passed down from generation to generation. In our parents' or grandparents' day women did not have the ability to open a bank account or take out lines of credit. It wasn't until the 1960s where a woman could open up a bank account for herself and not until the Equal Credit Opportunity Act (ECOA) of 1974 that women could have access to their own credit cards, car loans, and mortgages. The all-in method was the most common for years because of these laws. Today, I often see this setup when couples are young and starting out, maintain a one-income household, have a background or religious beliefs with this method, or one partner does not want any responsibility with money. By combining all assets in one place people feel that they are able to work 100% as a team on all financial decisions including spending, saving, and investing.

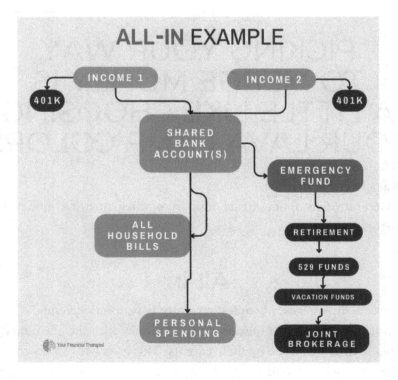

As with almost all things, there are pros and cons to choosing the all-in option.

Pros

- There is only one account to manage.
- You can see all your assets in one account.
- You are working on all goals together.
- There is financial transparency.

Cons

- If only one person is reviewing the account, the other person could be unaware of patterns (good and bad) or overspending leading to credit card or other debt.
- It's hard to surprise a partner with gifts :).
- Two people are pulling funds from the same account and if there is a lack of communication, overdrawing can happen.
  - This recently happened to a client when her husband paid for a weekend away for her birthday without telling her. The account went down to $40 without her knowing and she had a bill set on autopay that was about to be paid the next day.

Tip: When funding your hobbies from joint accounts, set a spending limit with your partner. For example, agree to discuss any purchases over $200 beforehand. This practice fosters trust and promotes fairness in shared finances.

Yours, Mine, Ours: Various Ways to Share Expenses and Spending Mindset

I like them, but I am not ready to go all in with money. I have my own banking setup and feel more comfortable with having some control over "my money."

This is when the yours, mine, ours setup can be the right solution for you.

- More than half of American couples (57%) have at least some separate financial accounts, including a mix of joint and separate accounts (34%) or completely separate finances (23%). Forty-three percent have only joint accounts.[6]

The following three steps for the yours, mine, ours options are also the steps to follow for the this-or-that, 50/50 split, and percentage of earning method options that come next:

1. Create a household spending, savings, and investing spreadsheet.
2. Identify who will pay; for example, is this an ours or theirs expense?
3. Be clear and write down exact dollar amounts needed for the ours savings, spending, investing plan by each person.

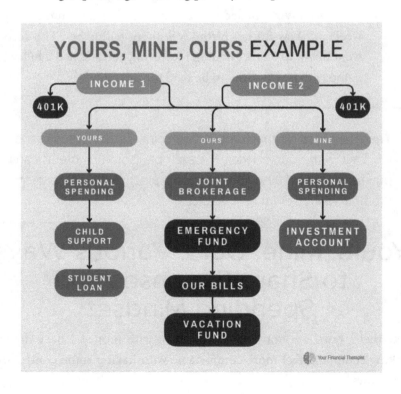

Merging Money and Mindsets with a Lover

This or That

Madison and José

Madison and José have fallen into this category naturally. Over their time dating and then José moving in, they started to do this ad hoc, but now with a baby on the way it was time to outline what will work proactively for them in the future.

Madison was already paying for her own bills, and didn't see a big deal of combining money, but José was thinking otherwise. He makes more money than Madison and once she has the baby her income will decrease (although hopefully not stop). The plan is to have his mom help babysit while Madison works a few mornings a week, otherwise Madison will be working weekend shifts while he is home leaving them with not a lot of family time, which comes at a different cost.

With the this-or-that method the higher income partner can cover more expensive bills, and the person who makes less can cover smaller items. It's great for couples with drastically different pay ranges, or if both parties have individual strengths in managing a particular area of the family finances.

For example, José covers the entire rent, both car payments/gas, and the grocery bill while Madison covers heating, cell phone, nights out (something she still wants to keep doing monthly), and health insurance, as well as home furnishings here and there.

Pros

- Each person contributes to the lifestyle in their own way.
- There is a sense of responsibility for the bill they "own."
- Together they can have a greater lifestyle.

Cons

- Financial bullying, when the higher earner feels they are able to control the financial decisions, can occur.

- There is a loss of financial intimacy as each person is working separately paying bills.
- Smaller bills often fluctuate from month-to-month, unlike rent, which is a fixed expense each month, and therefore at the end of the year it is recommended to do an annual view of spending to ensure the total number is within your expected budget for both of you.

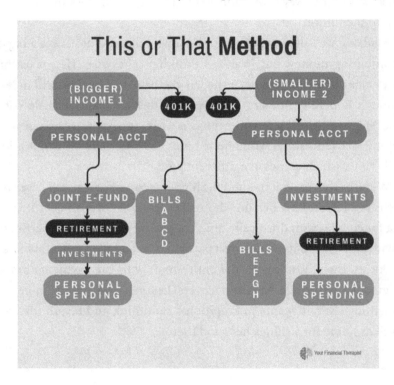

The 50/50 Split

Sophia and William

Keep separate accounts, but make equal payments into ours account.

Sophia and William currently make similar salaries, about $100K. (Yes, Sophia gets married! We will learn more about their money mindset

Merging Money and Mindsets with a Lover

in Chapter 5. For now let's use them in this example of splitting joint finances and household chores in half.)

They went through the first three steps and identified what was in the ours category of household expenses, savings, and investing, including a summer home for retirement.

The conversation went well overall, but they did have a few line items that needed to be discussed in more detail, such as how to split groceries when William's two sons stay with them every other week. (See Script 6: Blending Family, Financials, and Food.)

After doing the math on expenses and joint savings, they wanted $7,000 to put into the shared household accounts each month.

Combined Numbers	Individual Numbers
Gross income: $200,000	Gross income: $100,000
Net income: $130,000	Net income: $65,000
Monthly income: $10,800	Monthly take-home pay: $5,400

Sophia + William will each contribute: $3,500 to the ours account
$5,400 − $3,500 = $1,900 each with money left over each month to spend, save, or invest in the mine accounts.

For William this will be where his child support and college savings for the kids will come from, while Sophia will start a nest egg for possible IVF treatment if she needs it in the future. All of these things they discussed during the initial conversation on what was included in the ours, yours, and mine columns.

Pros

- This choice feels "fair" that each person is contributing the same to maintain their joint lifestyle.

- They are both working toward joint goals together while also keeping financial independence.
- They enjoy a shared sense of responsibility for savings, spending, and investing.

Cons

- The lower earner has less mine money each month/year.
- Different spending habits can lead to frustrations and/or resentment; for example, if one person is a saver, when it comes to retirement one partner has built a large nest egg while the other person did not plan for the same type of comfort in old age.
- This could be challenging when an unexpected bill arises or is greater than normal how and who will pay the difference.

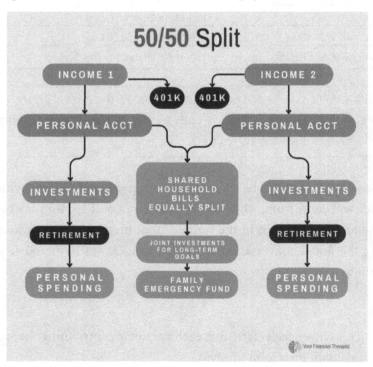

Merging Money and Mindsets with a Lover

Percentage of Earning Method

Averi and Sam

Averi and Sam have a wage difference, and Sam already has paid off much of the mortgage. They are exploring how to merge money using the percentage of earnings method to see if this will be a good fit for them.

Averi's gross income is $220,000	Net income: $145,000
Sam's gross income is $120,000	Net income: $84,000
Total gross income for the household: $340,000	Net income: $229,000

Averi brings home a larger salary and therefore will pay 63% of all the bills.

Sam will pay 37% of all the bills if we go by the exact dollar amount. While reviewing the numbers, they decided to go ahead with a 60/40 split that will make it easier to calculate bills each month.

They will create one joint account that they each contributed a percentage of the bills to and then whatever is leftover goes into their personal accounts.

For example, the electric bill is $200 for the month. Averi will pay $120 and Sam $80.

They will do this exercise for all expenses each month. As some bills fluctuate, I recommend having a 10% contingency line item in the spending budget to allow for months that there is overspending to ensure you do not go into overdraft because all bills aren't the exact same each month.

Pros

- There is equity in contribution based on income, making it more fair to both parties.
- There is flexibility that as income changes, the percentages also will change.
- This allows for shared financial account and goals and individual accounts for personal spending, savings, and investing.

Cons

- It requires complex calculations each month.
- If one partner has significantly more disposable income after contributing to the joint account, it could lead to feelings of imbalance or resentment.
- Conflict can arise when there is a difference in lifestyle, such as one person is frugal and the other is an overspender, in joint bills. Often the higher income earner feels they have the final say versus a joint decision.

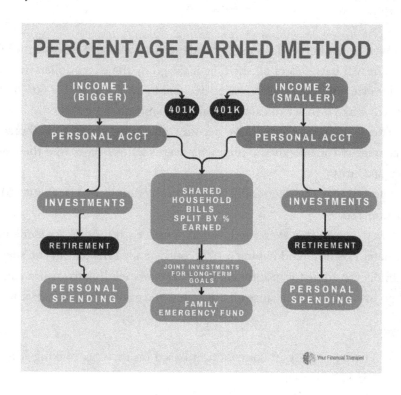

M = Make conversations comfortable

O = One by one

N = Nurture shared goals

E = Evaluate practical solutions

Y = Yes to compassion

Sam was ready to "host" the financial meeting because she was ready to plan not just the trip to California but also for a life together. For Sam, her favorite spot is in the breakfast nook on Sunday morning with light jazz playing and a warm cup of coffee and a blanket on her lap daydreaming of the day, week, month ahead. While this might be Sam's favorite spot, it is not what is best for the couple to talk about finances. Why, you ask? Because this is Sam's home, she would have home field advantage and by having Averi over to talk about finances could have Averi feeling like the visiting team.

When working with others, you need to take into consideration all the people involved to create an open environment. While one of you might be a morning person and the other is a night owl, talking about money at either of these times is not going to be best for you as a couple. Pause here and brainstorm for a minute. When and where have you connected and had meaningful conversations (outside of pillow talk)? The goal now is to try and re-create the same atmosphere. The time of day is important, so is the day of the week, temperature of the room, lighting, and noise levels around you.

Averi was excited about the upcoming trip to California. In her head she was paying for it all as she's the one who makes more money and she hates the feeling of owing anyone anything, even her partner. So on a recent road trip she was surprised when Sam brought up the vacation and spending conversation.

Madison and José are ready to have a conversation about finances, family, and the future baby on the way. Since neither of them have seen this successfully done, they didn't know where to start. Having worked through the Money Mindset Method recently to get out of credit card debt, Madison took the lead and asked José to print out his paycheck statement and block out Tuesday night after work.

CONVERSATIONS WITH YOUR FINANCIAL THERAPIST

Let's pull back the curtains and look inside the conversations that Averi and Sam and Madison and José are having regarding how to merge money in their relationship.

Tip: Go for a drive or walk, being side by side often makes conversations easier than sitting across from one another. This physical aspect of the conversation often reduces confrontation and encourages openness and problem-solving.

Averi and Sam	Madison and José
Leaving a family BBQ, Sam decides to bring up the subject of the upcoming trip to California while Averi is driving. This will allow Averi to focus on the road, let her guard down a little, and share her thoughts on the hour drive. Sam opens the window a crack for some fresh air and turns the music off.	Madison selected Tuesday night as her roommate works late that day. She prepared an easy dinner that night (she didn't want either of them to be hangry), printed out her latest spending sheet she kept and paycheck stub, and set the table.

M = Make conversations comfortable

O = One by one

N = Nurture shared goals

E = Evaluate practical solutions

Y = Yes to compassion

Tough conversations can help you become self-aware and reveal blind spots. It can also create a lot of unexpected emotions to arise. You cannot boil the ocean in one meeting. Remember that creating financial intimacy will take time, space, and patience. Just like with sexual intimacy, you don't try everything all at once; it happens over time and with some trial and errors. Start simple, something you both know you have a goal of, stay focused

Merging Money and Mindsets with a Lover

during your meeting, slow down, enjoy the time together while digging into learning more about each other's financial values, goals, and visions. As you grow your relationship and confidence in working together, add in more complex topics. Know at any point you can use the Money Mindset Method to guide you through those possible uncomfortable situations.

Tip: Create a code word to use when you know the conversation is no longer being productive. This can be a silly word that you both agree on to use when you need to take a break and regroup later. When you come up with the word, also come back with how and when you will come back to the conversations. (See Script 5: The Codeword Is _____.)

Here are some examples from clients:

- Code word: dance party. They have to hit the dance party button (yes, an Instagram impulsive purchase that they fought over, but now will have a purpose in their home). After the two-minute dance party they sit back down to talk it through with new energy.
- Code word: palm tree. For this couple it means one of them needs to get outside and go for a walk. They set a timer for 15 minutes and each takes a break to regroup, pause, reflect, and reset.

Leaving the conversation and coming back to it can be useful because brain breaks are good for several reasons, including increased blood flow to the brain, which helps with focus and attention. Moving your body shifts your breathing and often leads to new ways of thinking about a problem.

CONVERSATIONS WITH YOUR FINANCIAL THERAPIST

Averi and Sam	Madison and José
California has been a dream trip for Sam, and Averi is keen to make her dreams come true. Averi is planning a seven-day trip to California including hotel, airfare, meals, and wine tours. Sam's role will be to review the plan, add in any additional places, and make sure Averi doesn't overbook them. Starting with a smaller decision like a vacation felt like a good place to practice the Money Mindset Method before tackling moving in together. **Code word: DD** Short for the designated driver, the conversation was going all over the place and they needed to take a break.	Coming up with a clear path on bills, responsibilities, and savings goals was all important to the young couple: • Where will they live? • Can they afford to stay in Madison's place without a roommate? • Where will the baby sleep? • How much is a new car? • What is childcare going to cost? • How much is it to have a kid? • What much does José make? • What's in savings for Madison? • Does José have credit card debt? • Who will pay the grocery bill? • Who will pay the heating bill? • The baby has doctor appointments, right? What's that going to cost? **Code word: Pickles** A current pregnancy craving :).
Topic: How can we take a shared vacation and each feel financially comfortable?	**Topic:** What is the best way to financially support our new family in a safe environment without going into debt with all these changes around us happening?

M = Make conversations comfortable

O = One by one

N = Nurture shared goals

E = Evaluate practical solutions

Y = Yes to compassion

This is a good opportunity for the couples to align on their financial values and clarify the future goals for themselves as a couple. Now that you

Merging Money and Mindsets with a Lover

have a question or problem to solve, the next step is to find out why this issue is important to each of you through the step, N = nurture shared goals. Having a common why to solve the problem will help you both stay focused on finding a solution, staying on track, and reaching your goals as a team.

Averi and Sam	Madison and José
Averi has set aside $3,500 for this trip and didn't plan to ask Sam for anything. Sam doesn't feel comfortable going away with her partner and not contributing at all. She doesn't want to be seen as taking advantage of her kindness. It doesn't feel good.	The couple want to live in a safe neighborhood. Right now that includes a house with Madison's roommate. They want to provide their baby with food, diapers, and cute toys. They need a crib and a place for the baby to sleep. They need a reliable car. Does it make sense to sell a car or keep both? They do not want to go into credit card debt—for Madison that was really important as she just came out of debt.
Common goal: To spend time together creating amazing memories where they both contribute value to the trip.	**Common goal:** To provide a safe home within their means for their growing family.

M = Make conversations comfortable

O = One by one

N = Nurture shared goals

E = Evaluate practical solutions

Y = Yes to compassion

The goal of this step is to take the time to brainstorm ideas, share thoughts, research resources, and ask questions to seek a solution. It often creates an opportunity for growth as individuals and as a couple by working together to problem-solve and possibly learn a new skill, tool, or information along the way.

> **Tip:** Take out a piece of paper and your phone and set a timer for 10 minutes. Sit down and go: write down separately at first the areas and ways to explore your options. Then set the timer again and share your ideas giving each other five minutes of time. Put a check mark next to the ideas you want to come back and revisit together. Assign an owner and timeline of when to have it completed to avoid confusion of who is doing what next.

Averi and Sam	Madison and José
Sam wants to use her credit card miles for airfare. This means the flights Averi found won't work, but she is willing to compromise as they are still flying the same days.	Keeping a roommate could be helpful right now. The baby can sleep in their room. That will give them 12–24 months to save money to find their own place.
Averi enjoys wine-pairing dinners, and offers to pay for that for two nights. Sam agrees as long as she can do a picnic lunch that she can pack for them on two afternoons at a local park.	Sell one car and put that money into an emergency fund. Pick up a second job with Uber for four months on days Madison isn't working at the coffee shop to add to the baby fund. She will be off her feet and in a cool car.
The hotel was the next problem to solve. Averi has on her plan five nights at a B&B which will cost $350/night: $1,750 total. Sam is not okay with having her partner spend this amount on her.	If they get married, Madison can go on José's insurance before she delivers the baby. José feels it's important to him to pay the full rent amount.
The compromise was Averi will pay for three nights at the B&B and three nights they will stay at a less expensive option that Sam's friend recommended. To feel like she is also contributing, they decided that Sam will pay for those three nights.	Madison would like to keep some financial freedom as well, but is not sure how to do that.

Merging Money and Mindsets with a Lover

10 TIPS FOR PLANNING A TRIP TOGETHER

1. **Discuss your goals:** Talk about what you each want from the trip—relaxation, adventure, culture, or a mix.
2. **Choose a destination together:** Pick a spot that matches both your interests and travel preferences.
3. **Set a budget:** Agree on how much you're comfortable spending and stick to it. This number does not need to be the same dollar amount for each person. Set a number that you can financially afford. You can get creative and prioritize how and where you spend it when planning.
4. **Divide responsibilities:** Assign tasks, like booking flights, accommodations, or researching activities, to share the workload.
5. **Be flexible:** Build an itinerary but leave room for spontaneity and relaxation. Add in a small amount for a sunshine fund, which is unexpected expenses that pop up while on your trip that you want to splurge on—an extra ice cream or bottle of wine.
6. **List priorities:** Define what is most important to you on the trip. The location of the hotel or the bed sheet thread count? Money being spent on adventure activities or fine dining? Once you know where and how you want to spend your money and your time, you can plan appropriately for everyone to leave the holiday feeling good.
7. **Compromise on details:** Meet in the middle on preferences, like activities or dining choices, to keep things balanced. For example, one day of off-road four-wheeling and one night of dancing under the stars on the beach.
8. **Plan for downtime:** Don't overbook; leave time to relax and enjoy the trip stress-free and allow for the ability to embrace unexpected moments.

9. **Prepare for the unexpected:** Discuss how you'll handle delays, cancellations, or disagreements while traveling beforehand. Some people like to be in charge of handling the situation while others rather not to be involved. Knowing the roles each of you will play will help avoid a future fight.

10. **Embrace the experience:** Focus on having fun and learning about each other—it's about creating memories together! Live. Laugh. Love. You will leave the vacation with memories that made you laugh, cry, and want to do it again (hopefully!).

M = Make conversations comfortable

O = One by one

N = Nurture shared goals

E = Evaluate practical solutions

Y = Yes to compassion

Saying yes to compassion when merging money with a new romantic partner is essential because money is deeply tied to emotions, values, and past experiences. Compassion enables you to approach sensitive financial conversations with understanding and empathy, creating a safe space to share openly. It helps you navigate differences in spending habits, debt, or financial goals without judgment, fostering trust and cooperation. By prioritizing kindness, you can focus on building a partnership that respects both individuals' needs and strengthens your relationship. Merging money isn't just about finances—it's about aligning your lives, and compassion is key to making that process successful.

Merging Money and Mindsets with a Lover

Averi and Sam	Madison and José
Sam recognizes that travel can be stressful, and Averi likes order. If there is a change in plans she knows she will need to be patient and take deep breaths. (Good thing she has started taking yoga classes.) She can also provide a source of strength for Averi, who will learn she can lean on Sam during this unknown period while they wait to find out the new flight times and connections. Averi likes a plan, but also knows she will need to go with the flow as each day won't go as planned. She needs to be compassionate with herself to enjoy the moment as it is versus what it was planned in her head. She needs to learn to remind herself that it is okay once in a while to let Sam lead her off the planned activities.	Oftentimes Madison and José have to stop one another and just pause. This is all new to them: living together, healthy money conversations, and pregnancy hormones all mixed together. They need to remind themselves that this is new and will take practice and that they have a lifetime of practice ahead of them. Recently José paid for his parent's cell phone bill without talking to Madison, which meant they had $200 less this month for their joint emergency fund they were building. While she was upset at first, they sat down and talked about why she was upset and how next time they could come up with a solution together. Madison showed compassion for José after she understood why it was important to him to pay the bill. They also came up with a new rule that they talk about any money being given to family members over $50 together in the future.

As you are merging money with a partner, be aware of your own stress levels and emotions. Taking care and understanding yourself helps you be more patient and communicate clearer with your partner.

You also want to set up healthy boundaries of when and where to talk about money, the tone you prefer to use and be spoken to in, and when you need a break (hello, code word), which will help build strong financial intimacy.

CONVERSATIONS WITH YOUR FINANCIAL THERAPIST

Where Are They Now?

Averi and Sam have been working on boundaries, trust, and building financial intimacy with Sunday financial date nights. They are now able to talk about smaller financial decisions with ease and even came up with these options for the upcoming trip:

1. Averi can pay for the entire trip, which will leave Averi feeling proud of paying for it all herself and not owing anyone anything.
2. Together they shared what is important to them and where they have the best resources (example: airline miles).
3. Split the trip 50/50 right down the middle.

Which One Would You Choose?

Averi and Sam went with option 2. California dreaming was just that: it was a dream of a trip. Averi and Sam both enjoyed the time together and appreciated all the conversations they had ahead of time about money so when they were actually on vacation they could relax and enjoy the moments. They both felt like they contributed to the holiday and can't wait to do it again.

Where Are They Now?

Madison and José are falling into a routine of living together and building financial intimacy on a daily basis with small decisions so when the bigger decisions come they will be ready for them (as much as one can be). After reviewing the options of merging money here are the three options they came up with:

1. I pay for this and you pay for that (this or that).
2. Madison will stop working and José will be the sole provider (all-in).
3. Equal partners in finances, chores, and child caring (50/50 split).

Merging Money and Mindsets with a Lover

Which One Would You Choose?

Madison and José went with option 1. They sat down together and went line by line on the expense they each had on their own and together. Next to each item they put an initial down as to who wanted to be responsible for paying that bill or savings account and why it was important to them. If there was an item neither of them cared strongly about, they put it into a neutral column and at the end split up the expenses to equal out for now. If Madison needs to reduce her work hours due to the baby, they can adjust, but now they have the tools to do just that.

Bonus Since Practice Makes Progress

The California trip was a success. Sam and Averi were both able to relax and enjoy the time together and even learned a few new things about each other. Now that they knew they could travel well together and make financial decisions together, it was time to rework the Money Mindset Method with the focus on merging money when they move in together. Being successful solving a small problem made them feel brave enough and confident enough to take on the bigger challenges of moving in together.

The following provides a brief outline of how they reworked the steps for the next financial discussion of moving in together.

M = Make conversations comfortable
Tuesday half-price wine night has turned into a weekly date night spot for them. It's quiet, low key, and comfortable.
On Sunday, Sam sent Averi a text message saying, "Let's use Tuesday night to talk about our moving in together plan." This gave Averi an opportunity to plan (and worry), but not be caught off guard.

CONVERSATIONS WITH YOUR FINANCIAL THERAPIST

O = One by one
Sam has dreamed of having a partner to live with, but she also worries about giving up half her closet. Will she have to add Averi to the mortgage? If she does, will it increase her interest rate to refinance? "How can I have Averi feel like an owner without her being an owner?" Averi is uncomfortable coming into someone else's space—the kitchen is already set up—the couch is picked out. "What am I doing here? None of this is mine." "I am paying $1,500 in rent now, if I move in do I pay the same amount or less and pay off my student loans or is that seen as selfish?" **Common theme:** Build a life together, share life's little moments while feeling like equals.

N = Nurture shared goals
Averi is struggling to not be in control of where they live and how to contribute financially that makes sense for both of them. She is finding herself pulling away both physically and emotionally to delay the conversations. Sam has noticed this also and is starting to feel rejected as if this means she doesn't want to move in together. Sam pauses and points to the posted note she placed in front of them that she wrote after they decided on their shared goal. It read: "How can Averi move into Sam's house and feel like an equal financially in the home?"

This action was meant to remind them to focus on their shared goal they were working toward by placing it in front of them to be a visual reminder of the goal.

Together they took a deep breath knowing they were a team and ready to start the next step in the method.

Merging Money and Mindsets with a Lover

E = Evaluate practical solutions

"We should meet with an attorney to see about creating a document on financial rights to the house. That way I can keep my equity to date, and you feel like you are also contributing to our home financially."
- Sam can pay for the mortgage and Averi can pay for the insurance, taxes, and upgrades to the house (this or that).

"We live separately. I don't want to feel like this isn't my home, or you can sell your place and we buy a new one together."
- They can redecorate the house so Averi feels more at home.
- Involve Averi in the decision-making on everything for their home, from what flowers go outside, to what time the front door lights go on.
- Split the mortgage 50/50 and all the other bills. Whatever past equity Sam built isn't overlooked and they just move forward as partners.

Y = Yes to compassion

Averi knows small acts of kindness goes a long way with Sam to show she values her. Before work Averi left a sweet note in the home they are building together.

Sam knows Averi worries about a lot of unknown what-if things, so reassuring Averi is important in their relationship. Sam often reminds Averi that she is committed to making her feel valued and needed in their home together with words of affirmation weekly.

Where Are They Now?

Averi and Sam are still going strong and are enjoying living together. After a few bumps in the road, nothing abnormal for new couples starting to cohabitate, they have settled into a nice routine. Sam is enjoying packing lunches before work for both of them and Averi is loving the short commute and of course the extra time together.

They came up with three options:

1. Meet with an attorney to create a document that outlines what equity each other currently has and in the future if they sell.
2. Redecorate the home and Averi will pay the "other expenses."
3. Sell the house and buy something new together.

What Would You Do?

Once again they went with option 2. *(Teaser, you will wish they did option 1 later in the book.)*

Averi set aside $20,000 to redecorate the house starting with the new paint for the living room, fresh linens in the redone bathroom, and a new stove to cook on! Having her feel like a little of her was in the home made it more comfortable for both of them to call AS home. The new name they gave the place—AS is for Averi and Sam.

Merging Money and Mindsets with a Lover

MONEY MANTRA

I am wealthy, focused, and empowered.
I am and have enough.
I trust my decisions and honor my growth.
Every step I take builds freedom, abundance, and peace.

XOXO, Your Future Self

DO YOU BELIEVE IN CONSOLIDATING DEBT WHEN MARRIED
OR
KEEPING IT SEPARATE?

WHY?

SOURCE: LET'S TALK FINANCES CONVERSATION CARDS

CHAPTER FIVE

FROM DIAPERS TO DOG HAIR

THE OVERWHELMING JOY (AND EXPENSE) OF GROWING YOUR FAMILY

CONVERSATIONS WITH YOUR FINANCIAL THERAPIST

The money pie stays the same, yet the needs/wants/savings will change.

This chapter features Sophia and her new husband, William, and Gabe, who is adjusting to city living.

Sophia meets William when she is 40 years old. William is divorced with two sons. While they are happy as a family of four from the outside, Sophia is not confident in her role as a stepmom, always feeling a little out of the loop, which keeps reminding her that she really wants to have a biological child herself.

Gabe is working like crazy for what feels like 100 hours a week, yet he is feeling lonely when he does finally come home. He has not had a chance to make friends or go out exploring the city, leaving him in his free time wondering what to do and whom to do it with. He is thinking of getting a dog to come home to at night and explore the city with. They are called man's best friend for a reason, right?

Script 7: The Stroller Showdown: Function Versus Fashion

Script 8: New Additions, New Equations?

Script 9: Ruff Decisions: Exploring Dog Ownership

Get ready to scream—with excitement or fear or both! The roller coaster of life is about to take a twist and a turn, so hold on! For some, adding a new addition is both a treasured moment and a stressful one, especially when it comes to finances.

As you enter this next phase of your life it is an important time to review your finances both for yourself and as a family. This chapter will cover expanding your family and that can look different for people: from adding babies, kids, step-kids, grandkids, and/or pets. For this section let's focus on the cost of adding a child to the family either biologically, through blended families, adoption, foster care, or by family emergency where you are now the caregiver.

Most people think that adding a child in the early years is the most expensive phase with childcare costs, but kids grow up and so do their expenses, with new hobbies, social activities, and cell phone plans to name a (very, very!) few. I remember thinking I was going to be able to save money when I was done paying for preschool, but boy was I wrong. A friend with older children warned me about this as her daughters were involved in competitive dance, cheerleading, and social activities (hello, birthday parties) and that the savings you think you will have will disappear in new ways, and she was right. Thankful for the advice, I was aware of this shift and had a plan to find a way to split the difference by finding activities in town with low costs until my daughters found their passion and I put half the money aside for savings.

EXPANDING MONEY: KEY CONSIDERATIONS

At this stage of life, expenses are bound to increase, which can highlight potential differences with your partner when it comes to spending, savings, and investing. For instance, one of you might prioritize splurging on the latest, high-end stroller (See Script 7: The Stroller Showdown: Function Versus Fashion.), while the other is perfectly content with a second-hand option from a friend. Also, managing your time between personal life, work, and your new addition could affect your income and financial priorities. The key to navigating these changes successfully is maintaining open and ongoing communication. Regularly discussing your goals, values, and budget will help you stay aligned and tackle financial challenges as a team, which can be tricky with lack of sleep, change in patterns, and lots

CONVERSATIONS WITH YOUR FINANCIAL THERAPIST

of unknowns. The earlier you start these conversations and change in patterns, the easier it will be in the long run when you're exhausted and potentially very frustrated.

Just like when you start a new hobby, you start with simple and small movements repetitively. The same is true here with financial conversations and using the Money Mindset Method. Using the method frequently for smaller financial decisions will help prepare you for the larger conversations like adding a child for Sophia and William or deciding if Gabe is ready to be a dog dad.

* * *

After years of feeling like she would be alone forever, William stumbled into Sophia's life right around her 40th birthday; it almost felt like the Cinderella moment. Sophia's career in graphic design is going nicely and she and William have similar salaries. Together they have a healthy relationship, each taking time to listen to one another, making each other feel like equals, and prioritizing time together. They also continue to build their financial intimacy with scheduled financial meetings weekly to stay focused on the family goals big and small.

William's first marriage didn't have the same healthy, open communication on sensitive topics such as kids and money, which has made him overly open and honest in his relationship with Sophia. He left the first marriage with financial trauma from lack of financial trust as he was surprised when going through the divorce process to find out "they" had $75,000 in consumer debt he wasn't aware of; he swore he would never be in that situation again.

For William, his role as a father to his two teenage sons involves child support, college savings, and cars to pay for. The boundary Sophia and William have in place for "his kids and his finances" is that William pays for those line items from his money account, and he takes pride in supporting his children. This was all good until he and Sophia decided it was time to have a child together. Sophia has been fine with the way this has been working out, so when the topic of in vitro fertilization (IVF) came up she wasn't surprised with the outcome of the conversation.

From Diapers to Dog Hair

THE COST OF EXPANDING A FAMILY

Sophia and William

For Sophia and William expanding their family will be a costly one even before the little one arrives. The estimated average cost per IVF cycle is about $12,000, according to the American Society for Reproductive Medicine (ASMR) and can go up to $25,000.[1] With the average of two to three cycles before conception, that can be an investment in a range of $24,000–$75,000 for a couple. William was not 100% on board with spending this money on conceiving a child with IVF when he already has two children from his prior marriage that cost him nothing to make. After years of trying and seeing her friends struggle with infertility, Sophia knew this was her best chance to have a baby. She took $25,000 out of her savings, and started the process. On top of the cash requirement for IVF, there were missed days of work for doctor appointments, hours of sitting in waiting rooms with emotions running high, and let's not talk about the mood swings, hunger, and exhaustion that came with the process. Lucky for Sophia, it took one round to conceive, $22,000 from her savings, and nine months of preparing for motherhood.

The next conversation Sophia and William needed to have as a couple was how adding a new baby to the family would affect their spending, savings, and investing. They are currently using the 50/50 split method. Will this make sense in the next chapter of their life? (See Script 8: New Additions, New Equations?) Sophia recently discovered that, according to US Department of Agriculture data and inflation statistics from the Bureau of Labor Statistics for middle-income families with two children, raising one child in 2023 could cost an average of $331,933 from the time a child is born to age 18.[2] That breaks down to about $15,000–$18,000 a year. This does not include college tuition costs. Bottom line, kids are expensive.

Gabe

Meanwhile, Gabe is kicking ass at work, enjoying the freedoms of living in New York City, yet struggles with work–life balance and is starting to notice he is feeling lonely since his roommate moved out last year. The apartment is quiet and he has no one to talk to when he finally makes it home after a long day. The gnawing feeling of buying a dog is starting to grow. It would feel so good for him to come to someone who is excited to see him, snuggle on the couch together on cold nights, and listen to him share his day, and also whom Gabe is responsible for in his personal life.

Buying a dog can cost $500–$3,000+ from breeders or pet stores, with initial expenses like vaccinations and spaying/neutering adding another $500–$1,000. Each year in the United States, two to three million dogs are purchased, and about 3.1 million dogs enter shelters; only two million are adopted.[3] Adoption is a more affordable option, typically costing $50–$500, with fees often covering vaccinations, spaying/neutering, and microchipping. Unconditional love does come at a price. The initial cost of the dog is just the beginning of the expenses. Let's guide Gabe through the expenses of expanding his family by possibly adding a dog to the mix.

REBALANCING YOUR SPENDING, SAVING, INVESTING

Shifting expenses when a new family arrives is often challenging especially when you are going from a self-focused budget to now providing for something that is 100% reliant on you to stay alive. Your spending will

From Diapers to Dog Hair

automatically shift to the new needs of the family member, but how will you reduce or shift the other expenses that you were used to spending on? If you don't take the time to shift the expenses from one area to another you will likely end up in debt.

Before the new arrival, whether human or animal, it is suggested that you go over your current spending, savings, and investing, and highlight the areas that can or will change in the upcoming months. If possible, start living your new spending patterns before the new arrival comes home to help with the adjustment period as so many things will be changing at one time. This will also enable you to adjust any spending patterns that need adjusting or save a few months into an emergency fund for the little one. It's just a matter of time before an unexpected emergency room visit; take it from this mom of three!

M = Make conversations comfortable

O = One by one

N = Nurture shared goals

E = Evaluate practical solutions

Y = Yes to compassion

Sophia and William	Gabe
William usually spends Sunday morning golfing, and Sophia uses the time to go for a run. They meet up near lunch time to connect each week. Since both are usually feeling relaxed and ready for conversation, they have decided the first Sunday of the month will be their "money date."	Time to sit down with a pencil and paper and go through the Money Mindset Method. Gabe turns on his favorite playlist, pours a steaming cup of coffee, and sits down at the kitchen table on a chilly Saturday morning, nursing a slight hangover from the previous night.
This also includes saying no to other invites from friends, putting their phones in silent mode, and creating a safe space.	
Sophia and William made the decision to meet to talk about money each month. But it was easy to lose track of the many conversations they wanted to have, so Sophia created a calendar appointment in their phones with themes each month.	

CONVERSATIONS WITH YOUR FINANCIAL THERAPIST

Sophia and William	Gabe
Tip: She set it up once, repeating annually. Jan—New year goals Feb—Summer travel March—Retirement April—Raising kids	

M = Make conversations comfortable

O = One by one

N = Nurture shared goals

E = Evaluate practical solutions

Y = Yes to compassion

Begin discussions with straightforward questions, not looking for answers right now. Just list all the questions that come to mind. Find one topic, theme, or problem to focus on at a time. Keep this list handy for future conversations or meetings. Today's exercise is to focus on one area. This clarity helps keep conversations on track and ensures a deeper understanding and problem-solving.

Do you know how to eat an elephant?

One bite at a time.

The same is true here.

Sophia and William	Gabe
Sophia finds herself tossing and turning at night, worrying about what new financial issues could happen when the baby arrives.	Gabe had a lot of unanswered questions in his head so he put them on paper:

96

From Diapers to Dog Hair

Sophia and William	Gabe
Sophia's questions: How much time off from work will I need? Can we get a night nurse? I love my sleep. Who will be responsible for the baby's health care cost? How much is a nanny or childcare for a newborn? If William pays for his son's college, does that mean he isn't going to have enough to contribute to childcare when I want to go back to work? If he is always giving his kids everything, what do I/we get? William's questions: How will my sons feel about having a baby in the house? Can I afford another child? What about my golf game? I was just enjoying the kids being old enough to play with me. We are living in a nice neighborhood where rent is high, but close to my sons. Should we move outside the town for a few years to save money, or will my sons be upset that we moved?	Why do I want a dog so bad? How do I buy a dog? How much does it cost? Who will walk it when I am at work? How much is doggie daycare? What about travel? Who is a reliable person to watch the dog? Do I need doggie health insurance? Wow—that's a lot of questions!
Topic: We join them for the April discussion, planning for the financial, emotional, and lifestyle adjustments of adding a new baby to the family.	**Topic:** Does it cost to be a dog owner and am I ready for this responsibility?

M = Make conversations comfortable

O = One by one

N = Nurture shared goals

E = Evaluate practical solutions

Y = Yes to compassion

CONVERSATIONS WITH YOUR FINANCIAL THERAPIST

Sophia and William	Gabe
There are a lot of unknowns about what the future will look like with the new addition. The common ground concern for this process is how Sophia and William can raise the new child in a lovely and financially equal home in the next one to three years. **Note:** Staying focused on the short term will help drive the conversation to immediate actions. The two can revisit the process when looking at long-term goals because conversations about money are fluid and ongoing.	Gabe recognizes that he is lonely. Dogs are cute—and a lot of work. He has narrowed down the focus to the financial goal of what he can afford each month and an emotional goal for this process. The financial goal will be can he afford a dog for $400/month and will it fill the void of loneliness more than any headache it will cause trying to care for it.

M = Make conversations comfortable

O = One by one

N = Nurture shared goals

E = Evaluate practical solutions

Y = Yes to compassion

Sophia and William	Gabe
Financial boundaries are important to William since his prior relationship did not have enough. Together he and Sophia each came up with two ideas on how to shift spending from a duo to a trio Currently each put in $3,500 in a joint account = $7,000	Realistically can Gabe manage a dog? Sure. Whether this is a 14-year commitment he is ready for is another thing. He brainstormed ideas on how to get and maintain his future companion: • The pet store down the road always has dogs: cost $4,000.

From Diapers to Dog Hair

Sophia and William	Gabe

Researching that it will cost an estimated $1,500/month for the baby after birth, they brainstormed on what expenses they can shift without increasing the monthly amount.
1. Staying with the 50/50 expenses model:
  • Move to a less expensive rental outside the city. This will increase gas and travel time to work, but save $600 a month.
  • This will decrease their dining out as now they will be home more (savings of $350/month).
  • Reduce summer home savings by $1,000/month for the short term.
  • Sophia staying home reduces the need for a $1,500/month expense to $400, but that would also reduce their income in half.
  • Increase how much they each put into the joint account by $750/month, each to cover the expenses 50/50.
 	
2. Then they did the same exercise as if they shifted to the this-or-that method and came up with these four ideas:
  • Sophia will pay for the monthly childcare expense of $1,000.
  • William pays for the full mortgage $3,000 (that will increase his home payment $1,500), but he feels better paying for the mortgage in full than arguing over childcare expenses. Emotionally he is more comfortable with this.
  • Diapers and baby food go into the grocery budget, which Sophia picks up.
  • Baby classes go into activities and hobbies, which William pays for.
	• Rescue dogs seem cool, but I won't know what I am getting, which makes me nervous.
	• Having a dog will make me go for a run before work; that would be great for both of us.
	• What happens when I have late nights at work? Who will feed/walk the dog?
	• I can ask my neighbor sometimes, or hire a dog walker that my coworker uses for $30/walk. I need to set aside $150/month for dog walks.
	• Oh wait, I heard about doggie day care. That's $50/day. If I send him once a week, that's $200 a month.
	• My mom is allergic to dogs. What happens when I want to go home for the holidays? I'll just ask my sister who lives nearby if the dog can stay with her.
	• The pet store mentioned they sell pet insurance. I'll skip that; my dog will be healthy.
	• Gosh, I would love to feel uncondi-tional love.
	• I am working too much and can use a reason to leave the office.
	• Maybe I'll meet some friends at the dog park???
	• I could consider fostering a dog temporarily or pet-sitting to get a feel for the daily responsibilities without the long-term commitment.

M = Make conversations comfortable

O = One by one

N = Nurture shared goals

E = Evaluate practical solutions

Y = Yes to Compassion

Sophia and William	Gabe
S: "We're in this together, and we'll figure out the best way to manage our finances as a team. We can make adjustments as they come, as this is new for us. Mistakes will be made and there will be misunderstandings, so let's keep communication open and honest as we always do." **W:** "I'm grateful for how we're handling this as a team." **S:** "We're doing great planning for our baby's future together. If we keep this up, our baby will have a great future both emotionally and financially. Is it too early to start a retirement account for her?" (laughing)	Acknowledge that it's okay to have doubts and that feeling uncertain doesn't make me any less caring or capable. In fact, it will make me a better dog owner one day. Understand that no decision is perfect, and it's okay to change my mind later if circumstances change.

Where Are They Now?

After their April meeting, Sophia and William both realized that not just their life was about to shift for them with a new addition but also other parts of their relationship. They have had years of open and honest communication (aka practice) talking about money from small to major decisions, which was helpful for them to come up with three new ways to share expenses for them.

1. Moving to a this-or-that financial split enables each person to own expenses for the family.

2. Keeping with the 50/50 split and increasing their joint account from $7,000 to $8,000 reduces their mine accounts by $500 each month, along with reducing their eating out and subscriptions each month to cover the new expenses.
3. Go all-in—what the heck, we are married and keeping our expenses separate is too difficult right now to deal with.

What Would You Do?

They went with option 1 and also kept a joint savings account for future home projects, vacations, and that summer home one day; they each contribute $1,000/month into the joint account. They are enjoying their beautiful little girl, named Stella. She has changed their world for the better (other than the sleepless nights 😂). William's sons are also happy to have a little sister to dote on. It doesn't hurt that the high school girls love seeing them with her 😄. The prep work Sophia and William did ahead of time on the finances paid off as well both financially and emotionally because if they started this process after Stella was born, Sophia would not have the same patience as she did then with all the sleepless nights.

Where Are They Now?

Gabe is out for a walk on a cold winter day, pondering whether or not to get a dog. He is so glad he put the extra time into the decision-making process. While he thought he asked all the right questions, it turns out there were a few more he didn't even know about that have since popped up.

Here are the three solutions he came up with:

1. Dog sit for a coworker who was on assignment for six months.
2. Bite the bullet and buy the dog he saw in the window after work and "just figure it out." So many people are dog owners and he could do it, too.

3. Recuse a year-old dog who is housebroken and looking for love the same way he is. It would cost less and be doing a good deed.

What Would You Do?

Meet Spike, the rescue dog. Gabe went with option 3 and found the perfect dog for him. Spike is a mixed breed, found wandering the street and looking for love. While he is a handful, costing him $400 a month with doggie day care, a dog walker, and food, the two are in love (on most days). Recently though, Gabe came home late from work one day to find that Spike had eaten the Halloween candy that was out, and a quick trip to the emergency vet has him rethinking the pet insurance policy!

From Diapers to Dog Hair

MONEY MANTRA

I am wealthy, focused, and empowered.
I am and have enough.
I trust my decisions and honor my growth.
Every step I take builds freedom, abundance, and peace.

XOXO, Your Future Self

DESCRIBE WHAT A WEALTHY LIFE LOOKS LIKE FOR YOU NOW.

SOURCE: LET'S TALK FINANCES CONVERSATION CARDS

CHAPTER SIX

FROM OURS TO MINE

FINDING STABILITY IN FINANCIAL SEPARATION

CONVERSATIONS WITH YOUR FINANCIAL THERAPIST

This chapter features Madison and José, and Averi and Sam.

Splitting up is never easy to do. After 11 years of marriage, Madison and José have decided to go their separate ways. They have decided to divorce with dignity for their two children, who are now 11 and 6 years old.

Averi caught Sam cheating and is not happy. After several years of living together in Sam's home, Averi is now left to figure out how to heal from the relationship while finding a new place to live.

Script 10: Breaking Up and Breaking Even: The House That Was Ours

Script 11: Navigating and Collaborating a Divorce

Divorce is a death; at least it was to me. The only difference is no one brought over casseroles. While it was happening, especially the first few months, I felt very alone. Yet I am not alone; in fact, half of all first marriages end in divorce, with the average length of a first marriage being eight years.[1]

When two people get married or share a committed relationship, there are hopes and dreams that their relationship is built on: patterns of communication, eating meals together, and shared financial roles that all of a sudden (or like a slow death) it is all gone. A time of mourning is needed, yet you still need to work with your-soon-to-be ex-partner to divide assets and liabilities that were once shared dreams. This can be very emotionally draining and stressful, often leading to short-sighted financial decisions to "just get it over with" or overpaying attorney fees for fighting for what feels fair to one side versus what is mathematically correct. It has been shown that 90% of financial decisions are emotional and 10% logical.[2] Understanding and controlling your emotions will be an integral part of this stage.

Top reasons people get divorced:

- Infidelity
- Finances
- Communication
- Abuse (physical, mental, financial)
- Just grew apart
- Loss of intimacy and connection

It is no surprise to me that financial issues are one of the top reasons people separate. In society we are taught not to talk about money with others, yet when we merge our lives together often financial conversations are avoided or misunderstood. This often leads to resentment instead of respect for your partner. We each uniquely have a relationship with money based on our background, religion/culture, and personal experiences, which lead to different spending habits, values, and priorities. Without taking the time to understand your partner's financial mindset, disagreements and financial troubles brew.

DIFFERENT WAYS TO FACILITATE A DIVORCE

When I was going through the divorce process I went to the bookstore, desperate for guidance on how to get divorced with respect. But all I could find were books about getting even and not stopping at anything to achieve your end results. This was not the mindset I was in. I wanted to move on in the best way for both of us and most important for our very young children. It is nice to see over the decade since I went through the process that there is a new amicable way to divorce called *collaborative divorce.*

Collaborative divorce is a process where couples amicably negotiate their divorce settlement without going to court. Each spouse hires specially trained collaborative attorneys, and both parties commit to open communication and transparency. They often involve other professionals like financial advisors, financial therapists, and child specialists to address all aspects of the divorce as a team. A key feature is the "no court" agreement, requiring attorneys to withdraw if the process fails, incentivizing cooperation. In fact, 95% of collaborative divorces are settled in less than 12 months[3] versus 65% with the traditional divorce process.[4] This method aims for respectful resolutions, often saving time, reducing stress, and lowering costs compared to traditional divorce litigation.

Divorce can and will be unique to each couple. For example, the average cost range for a simple, uncontested divorce in Florida typically falls between $500 and $2,500, depending on various factors, and can be filed online in a matter of minutes all the way through a contentious divorce, which can take years and cost hundreds of thousands of dollars in attorney fees and emotional turmoil.

BREAKDOWN OF POTENTIAL COSTS OF DIVORCE IN FLORIDA IN 2025

Filing fees: $400–$410 (varies by county). This is a mandatory fee to file the Petition for Dissolution of Marriage.

Summons issuance fee: $10–$15

Mediation: If required, around $60–$120 per session for court-sponsored mediation. Private mediation can be between $100 and $500 per session.

From Ours to Mine

Sheriff or process server fee: $40–$75 to serve divorce papers.

Service by publication (if the spouse cannot be located): $200–$300 (includes newspaper fees).

Online divorce services: $150–$500 for minimal assistance with form preparation.

Attorney fees: For limited-scope representation or review of forms, costs typically range from $1,000 to $2,500 for an uncontested divorce. For a contested divorce, costs can range from $15,000 to $150,000 per spouse depending on the complexity.

Notary fees: Approximately $10–$20 if forms need to be notarized.

Parenting course fees: Required for divorces involving minor children; usually $25–$50.[5]

No matter how you and your partner use to divorce, as you go through this process you will have various people around you giving advice based on their expertise or personal experience. Your attorneys are looking out for your overall best interests from a legal standpoint, your financial advisor is looking out for your invested money, but who is looking out for your emotional triggers regarding splitting assets, everything from the airline miles, to the furniture, to the retirement plans? This is where you might need to build strength and resilience or ask for additional support. You don't have to go through this alone.

Breathe.

Breathe again.

And again . . . breathe.

Removing emotions from finance sounds easy until you are looking at the brand-new leather couch you recently spent hours deciding if you should splurge to buy. Now that it is broken in nicely, do you have to "give it away" or get a saw and split it in half (yes, that thought did cross my mind at one time)? Or do you keep it and give away the kitchen table instead? Oh wait, but that's where my kids have all their family dinner memories . . .

ahhhhh . . . . Emotions are everywhere in the separation process. Understanding your emotional triggers, building a mindful practice to reduce the noise, and focusing on the long-term goal will pay off in the long run for your health and wealth.

When you find yourself thinking of money or sitting in a divorce meeting and emotions are rising, pause and scan your body for stress showing up. Our bodies naturally are programmed to sense danger with our autonomic nervous system, making sure that we survive in moments of danger and thrive in times of safety. When we receive cues of danger we react, and when we receive cues of safety we relax.

Our body gives us signs when we feel our safety is in jeopardy. This can be a lion about to eat you in the wild to a financial discussion with your soon-to-be-ex-partner on child support. One technique to help calm the nervous system is to put your hand on the spot where emotions are showing up on your body and honor it. Start to listen to your body and learn your triggers. Is it when you hear words such as *always*, *never*, *can't*, and *forever*? Those are fixed words that do not allow for growth or opportunity and are generally used as threats versus realities in negotiation.

The end of a relationship can mean the end of fighting over money or having to compromise on expenses, but it can also bring the need to learn new skills and possibly redefine your relationship with money for your next life chapter.

It's common to feel overwhelmed when untangling finances, especially when a large part of your financial landscape has been linked to another person for so long. The process can stir up insecurities about the future, which may lead to self-doubt or fears about managing finances alone. These feelings might also be heightened if there's been a history of financial disagreements or if one partner was more financially dependent on the other. Facing these emotions and finding ways to address any lingering resentment is an important part of moving forward, as holding onto anger can make it difficult to reach fair financial agreements and start fresh.

From Ours to Mine

Your relationship with money has been with you since you were little and will continue to be with you until you die (and after—see Chapter 9), so now is the time to throw your shoulders back and metaphorically pick up the weights and start strengthening your financial knowledge and work in a growth mindset.

> "You cannot see your reflection in boiling water. Similarly, you cannot see the truth in a state of anger. When the water calms, clarity comes."
> —Author unknown

It's time to play the hype music, get out your fancy pens, set a timer, call a friend over, whatever you need to do to tackle a task you might not want to do, such as gathering your finances in one place. For most of my clients just starting the process of separating, this is often the task that is overwhelming to them. So I ask you,

How do you get an overwhelming task done? _____.

Apply the same tactic here.

For me personally, I need a big due date, short-term goals (today I am working on bank accounts for 30 minutes) with more immediate due dates, list reminders on my calendar, and music for dance breaks when my brain needs a rest.

Let's break it down into four tasks.

Task 1: Get organized. Gather key financial information in one place. Digitally create a folder to keep financial statements of all kinds: past taxes, estate plans, auto loans, bank and credit card statements, mortgage information, and more. Create a spreadsheet that lists all the financial information in one place for easy reference because you will have to refer to this information more than you think. If gathering this information together stresses you out, ask a friend or family member to sit down with you to do this work, put on a playlist, and knock it out. You can also print it all out and create a binder with this information to reference. (This was my preferred method—hello, big white binder. It went everywhere with me the first few months.)

Task 2: Understand what you own and what you owe. This means taking stock of everything you own—like your savings, investments, life insurance, long-term insurance policies, pensions, property, and any valuable assets (house, car, jewelry, etc.)—and being equally aware of what you owe, including debts, loans, and credit card balances. When you fully understand both sides, it becomes easier to set realistic financial goals, manage budgets, and make informed decisions. Being mindful of your assets and liabilities gives you the control and clarity needed to build a stable, confident approach to financial health. It also might come with a few surprises. Some of my clients started to look more into their finances and found missing money, accounts they didn't know about, and large sums of credit card debt. This is financial infidelity, which is when couples with combined finances lie to each other about money. Examples of financial infidelity can include hiding existing debts, excessive expenditures without notifying the other partner, and lying about the use of money. Unfortunately, when getting a divorce you are still responsible for these expenses, even if you did not know about them, unless you are able to work amicably with your ex to define what you are responsible for and what they are responsible for outside of the 50/50 split.

Task 3: Know what bills are due and protect your credit. Start by listing all your bills—both shared and individual—note due dates and responsibilities for paying. For personal bills, consider setting up automatic payments to avoid missed deadlines, and if you share expenses with your ex-partner, establish a temporary agreement on how to handle them to prevent any impact on both of your credit scores. Regularly monitor your credit report for any unexpected changes, as this can help you catch missed payments or new accounts early. Gradually separating joint accounts or transferring shared bills to individual names also minimizes future complications. By staying proactive and organized, you can protect your credit and financial well-being as you transition to managing finances on your own.

From Ours to Mine

If your partner isn't cooperating with bills and finances during a separation, it's essential to take steps to protect yourself and minimize the impact on your credit and financial stability. These actions tend to be motivated by power and control. This is not legal in any situation and although people think they can get away with it or you feel this can happen, legally it cannot. If your former partner refuses to contribute to bills, prioritize payments for essential services to avoid late fees and credit damage. Contact creditors to explain the situation and see if you can set up individual accounts or even freeze joint accounts to prevent any unapproved spending. You may also consider opening a new account in your name only to start fresh and have more control over your finances.

Finally, consulting a lawyer can provide guidance on securing your financial interests during the separation, especially if your partner is unwilling to cooperate. While it may feel overwhelming, each step you take now will help secure your financial independence and stability once the divorce is finalized.

Task 4: Create your go-forward budget. Creating a short-term budget during separation doesn't have to be overwhelming and can bring a lot of peace of mind during an uncertain time. Start by listing out your essential monthly expenses like rent or mortgage, groceries, utilities, insurance, and any loan or credit payments. Then, add any specific separation-related costs, such as moving fees, legal expenses, or setting up a new place. Take a look at shared expenses too—like child support or joint bills—and figure out what's reasonable for now. It's helpful to keep things simple: focus on the essentials, reduce unnecessary spending, and try to build a small emergency cushion if possible. A budget like this is meant to be flexible, so check in with it every month or so to adjust for anything new. This way, you can feel more in control and focus on what matters most in the transition.

Mistakes or setbacks are bound to happen. Yes, read that again. There can be a miscommunication on who was paying for the snow removal or quarterly home owners association (HOA) fees on bills that don't occur often to perhaps overlooking the need to change account beneficiaries or remove a partner's name from shared accounts, which could lead to confusion or unintended consequences later. Navigating financial separation also brings up the need for acceptance and patience with oneself, as mistakes or setbacks are bound to happen.

While managing finances independently may be new for some people, it's also an empowering opportunity to reshape one's relationship with money. Many find that facing these challenges leads to a renewed sense of control and financial literacy. Building confidence in handling money alone, exploring one's financial goals, and setting up a new path can be liberating, but it takes time. Acknowledging the emotional hurdles and finding a support system—whether through friends, family, or professionals—can provide strength, reminding you that, while it's difficult, this process is part of building a more resilient and independent future.

Madison and José

Madison and José are at crossroads in their relationship after 12 years together, married for 11 with two kids; their relationship has run its romantic course. When the conversation came up a few months ago, Madison and José agreed to separate as amicably as possible. But over the past few weeks it has turned in a different direction and the kids are noticing the tension in the house. José's mom, Marta, also isn't helping the situation. Although in the past few years she has warmed up to Madison, she is also very protective of her son. Once José's family started to get involved in the conversation of separating finances, the tension grew. Initially Madison and José wanted to go the collaborative divorce route, but will that be possible now with outside influences telling him to leave her with nothing?

Having done the Money Mindset Method many times before to help structure financial decisions, Madison recommended they sit down and do the same here.

From Ours to Mine

Averi and Sam

Averi and Sam are also at crossroads in their relationship, but not an amicable one. After eight years together, Sam has fallen in love with a colleague at work. This was something Averi was not prepared for and was shocked when she found inappropriate text messages on Sam's phone. She immediately kicked Sam out of the house, but later realized that Sam actually owned the house. (Recall from Chapter 4, they decided not to see an attorney to document the financial equity of the house but rather to share expenses moving forward. Yes, this decision has come back to bite both of them.) Averi considered AS their home, her home, a place she doesn't want to leave. Sam is the one who cheated and wants out of their relationship. Let her leave is Averi's mindset. Sam, however, is happy to move out for a little bit until emotions calm down for Averi. After all, it's Sam's name on the title and mortgage. She's moving back in no matter what!

After a few weeks have past, Sam approaches Averi to find a solution about separating more formally, including the house. Averi initially isn't interested, but after a few days agrees to meet to work through the Money Mindset Method to find a solution.

M = Make conversations comfortable

O = One by one

N = Nurture shared goals

E = Evaluate practical solutions

Y = Yes to compassion

During this stage of life, making a conversation comfortable might feel like anything but possible. Creating a comfortable space for a conversation with someone reluctant to talk requires patience, empathy, and creativity.

CONVERSATIONS WITH YOUR FINANCIAL THERAPIST

Madison and José	Averi and Sam
Kitchen table. Saturday morning. The kids are playing outside, which gives them a quiet house. They both turn their phones to silent, shut off the TV, and focus on one another. It was time.	Not a chance of sitting down with "her" was Averi's initial response, but days later when emotions cooled a bit they met at a neutral place—the local diner where they can sit down and have a conversation. Averi couldn't look Sam in her eyes the entire meeting, the hurt was too raw, but they were able to sit down at a table for an hour. (See Script 10: Breaking Up and Breaking Even: The House That Was Ours.)

M = Make conversations comfortable

O = One by one

N = Nurture shared goals

E = Evaluate practical solutions

Y = Yes to compassion

After years together there could be a lot of misunderstandings, assumptions gone wrong, resentment built up, and all the other emotions that come with the love of your life parting ways. This is not the time to bring those feelings to the table. This is the time to focus on what questions you have right now. Use the time to write down all the questions you each have separately. Then review the list and see what theme is common in both your lists. Keep the list of questions handy to allow you to set up another meeting in the future for other conversations that are needed. Today you will focus on one topic at a time.

From Ours to Mine

Madison and José	Averi and Sam

José wonders:
    How will they get divorced?
    Does each hire an attorney?
    Do it themselves?
    Work together?
    When will we tell the kids?
    How can the kids stay in their school?
 	
Madison wonders:
    Who will live in the house?
    Can one of them afford to stay
    there alone?
    How will time management work
    with the kids?
    What will they tell the kids? Their friends?
 	
Madison starts spinning with so many thoughts and fears. José is starting to feel overwhelmed.
 	
After a brief moment of feeling overwhelmed, they agreed to start over and start simple. One by one.
	"Just move out" are three words that sound so simple, yet separating their lives means so many things.
	
	Averi wonders:
	• Who will stay in the house?
	• If one person leaves, with what?
	    • Equity? Cash?
	    • Furniture?
	    • Nothing?
	• What will happen to the joint savings account?
	• The Christmas tree ornaments?
	• Plane tickets for the upcoming vacation back to California?
	
	Sam wonders:
	• Why am I not living in my home?
	• If she is living there, am I responsible for the HOA fee this month?
	• What's all this spending on our joint credit card?

Topic: How will they start the divorce process? What resources do we need as individuals and as a couple?	**Topic:** Who will stay in the house?

M = Make conversations comfortable

O = One by one

N = Nurture shared goals

E = Evaluate practical solutions

Y = Yes to compassion

You might have—who are we kidding—you definitely have a lot of differences right now but there is at least one common theme/topic/goal you both can work on together toward. Use this time to focus on that.

CONVERSATIONS WITH YOUR FINANCIAL THERAPIST

Madison and José	Averi and Sam
Here is what they come up after a shared brainstorm: • Get divorced. Period. • Put their kids first. • If possible keep the kids in their home (and school); they both want that. • Still like each other after this process is done. • Not fight over the little things like who gets the pots and pans. • Keep his mother (and outside influences) out of their divorce.	They agree on the following: • Sam put the down payment down for the house. • The mortgage is in Sam's name only. • Averi contributed $20K for renovations. • The mortgage for the past eight years had been split evenly. The house is close to Averi's office and she works late hours. Sam has already moved in with the new love interest. They both love the home equally. Financially Averi can afford to live there on her own while for Sam it would be a stretch as the homeowner's insurance has doubled since she bought the house along with all the other bills.
The shared goal is to navigate the divorce process amicably while prioritizing their children's well-being, maintaining a positive relationship with each other, and minimizing conflict over material possessions and external influences.	The shared goal is to reach an equitable resolution regarding the home they both value, taking into account their individual financial capabilities and future living arrangements.

M = Make conversations comfortable

O = One by one

N = Nurture shared goals

E = Evaluate practical solutions

Y = Yes to compassion

Seeking a solution can take some thinking outside the box. It might also involve letting go of the ego's desire to "win" and instead focus on what is fair for everyone involved.

From Ours to Mine

Madison and José	Averi and Sam
Now it is time to seek out solutions to their agreed common goals of getting divorced, putting the kids first, reducing outside noise, and still liking each other at the end of the process. They have seen many people around them go through the divorce process. Some went smooth and others lasted years, were super ugly, and cost thousands and thousands of dollars. They identify three possible solutions: 1. Fill out the documents themselves without outside counsel and "just figure it out." They are both adults. "It will be cheap and cheerful," says José. 2. Each gets their own attorney, lists all their assets, liabilities, desired time sharing for the kids, and leaves it up to the attorneys to fight it out. Downside with this one is they have seen their friends go this route and what starts off as equal splits turns very emotional and costly in the long run. Not something they both want. 3. Recently their neighbors used collaborative divorce attorneys and they are still friends and their kids seem well adjusted—let's ask them who they used and more about the process. (See Script 11: Navigating and Collaborating a Divorce.)	Averi wants to sell the house. If Averi can't stay in the house she made a home, sell it. Sam should move back into the house with her new partner or find a roommate to split the bills with. Averi walks away with nothing; after all, it's Sam's house. "Averi can have the couch and kitchen items," says Sam. Averi refuses to leave and hires a lawyer to fight for her rights to stay on the property. Averi can buy out the equity Sam put into the home initially and own it outright but then Sam doesn't get any money out of the house she has owned for years. When it sells in the future, if there is a gain she does not receive the profits. Consult a real estate attorney and ask for advice. Pay for the attorney out of their joint savings account.

M = Make conversations comfortable

O = One by one

N = Nurture shared goals

E = Evaluate practical solutions

Y = Yes to compassion

Emotions are high. Acknowledge ahead of time that you will make mistakes during this process. When it happens, learn from it, laugh about it, grow from it, and then release it.

Self-care is important during this phase of life. Take the time to do what you like, and find a bit of happiness in your daily/weekly routine.

Madison and José	Averi and Sam
Madison takes up yoga and José starts running again. Using the code word they created when she was pregnant (*pickles*) to know when they needed to take a break and reset a conversation has helped. Have compassion for others. If you see your soon-to-be ex-partner struggling on a day they have the kids, offer to take the kids from them for a few hours—it could be a win-win for both of you. You are both human and adjusting.	Averi joins a running club and starts training for a half marathon. It gives her something to do at night and make new friends in the area. Averi avoids going out to restaurants in her own neighborhood so she won't run into Sam with the new girlfriend. They both agree to remove each other from social media to protect their mental health. Sam writes Averi a letter of apology. While it didn't fix the hurt, it helped Averi understand a little bit more.

Where Are They Now?

Madison and José are divorced. They accomplished their shared goal to divorce and still be friends at the end of it. Madison is living in the house they used to share. José has moved into his Mom's home for the time being for two reasons: cheap rent with lots of space for his kids to have their own space, and he could help his mom around the house as he noticed she was slowing down a bit.

Here are the three options they reviewed:

1. Do an uncontested online divorce themselves and just figure it out.
2. Do a traditional divorce with two attorneys fighting it out.
3. Do a collaborative divorce that will allow them to work as a unit now and in the future.

What Would You Do?

After talking with both their neighbors, Madison and José decided to go with option 3. Their goal of working together and having a future relationship was important to both of them. Knowing that it was going to be an emotional process to split the furniture and finances, they went with the option that would provide the most support with less of a price tag in the long run. The professionals also helped support them both on keeping outside influences (hello, Marta) from distracting them from their goal of splitting up their lives fairly. The divorce cost them approximately $8,000 and was completed in six months.

Where Are They Now?

Sam and Averi had a rough few months trying to work out who would live where and how they would leave the relationship feeling whole financially.

After meeting at the diner they came up with these three options:

1. Averi moves out—takes the couch and kitchen appliances.
2. Sam sells the house and they both split the profits and start new.
3. They hire an attorney to calculate the dollar amounts Averi is due under common law rights, and Sam moves back into the home.

What Would You Do?

Averi ended up going with option 3. A friend in her law office referred her to an attorney who specializes in separation of common law property. It took a few months to work out the details, but in the end both Sam and Averi were able to come to an agreement, including paying for the legal fees from their joint savings account.

Sam is still with her new girlfriend living in her home. Averi has since gotten a promotion at work that allows her to live on her own. She found the perfect place with a cute garden.

From Ours to Mine

MONEY MANTRA

I am wealthy, focused, and empowered.
I am and have enough.
I trust my decisions and honor my growth.
Every step I take builds freedom, abundance, and peace.

XOXO, Your Future Self

CO-PARENTING EXPENSES WILL BE CHALLENGING

BECAUSE...

_____

_____

_____

SOURCE: LET'S TALK FINANCES CONVERSATION CARDS

CHAPTER SEVEN

RAISING TOGETHER, APART

CO-PARENTING WITH FINANCIAL CONFIDENCE

CONVERSATIONS WITH YOUR FINANCIAL THERAPIST

This chapter features Madison and José, and Sophia and William.

After being divorced for several years we will see how Madison and José navigate back-to-school shopping for their two children now ages 9 and 14 in a way that works for both parents' schedule off work and wallets.

Sophia and William divorced two years ago when Stella, their daughter, was 13 years old. Now Stella is 15 and a rising soccer star. Together they need to find an agreement on what team and how much to spend on her budding career.

Script 12: The Great Back-to-School Budget Debate

Script 13: Time for a Family Huddle

Script 14: The Game Within the Game: Tournament Logistics

Navigating the world of co-parenting brings its own set of adjustments— just like merging finances does. Over time, a child's needs, wants, and desires shift, often in unexpected ways, regardless of how thoroughly you mapped out a parenting plan at the start. Learning to communicate, respect, and appreciate each other's perspective can save hours of conflict, reduce personal stress, and, most important, create a more peaceful environment for the child. Kids are always watching and listening, even when we think they're not. So, if financial communication hasn't been easy, now is a great time to build this skill.

I have spent over 12 years co-parenting, and while we didn't always get it right, both of us work to keep the kids' needs front and center. The challenges were especially tough when our children were young, without the ability to voice their preferences or keep in touch independently with the other parent. Now that they're older, there's a different level of trust and a sense of shared responsibility over certain issues. It's still not always easy, but focusing on the big picture helps us prioritize the kids' needs over our own personal opinions or judgments.

Raising Together, Apart

Also, it is easy for triggers to flare up from past conflicts or unresolved feelings to creep into co-parenting discussions, making conversations tense or defensive. My tip here is to practice a "business-like" tone in communications, focusing on facts and needs over emotions, because this can help co-parents stay focused on what's best for their children. If you are having big emotions, it is best to send the text to a friend versus your ex, give yourself a time-out to cool down and when things feel too heated, taking a break. Using the code word if you had one from when you were married and returning to the conversation later can also help.

In co-parenting, decisions on finances can become more complicated without that mutual influence you might have had before separation. Working together for your children's best interests takes patience, flexibility, and clear communication—especially when the unexpected comes up, like back-to-school expenses, travel sports, or special events. One friend shared that whenever she needed to discuss finances outside the basics, her ex would simply respond, "Per the divorce decree." Since the parenting plan was set a decade earlier, anything beyond that list became her responsibility. This wasn't easy when things changed as their children grew up—suddenly, their original list of "predictable expenses" spiraled into a list of school projects, teacher gifts, summer camps, and endless other surprises. What began as a single text could quickly turn into a long series of heated messages, leaving everyone frustrated.

Without regular communication, these unforeseen expenses often cause strain on both co-parents and children alike. But regular check-ins—brief conversations dedicated to finances—can keep both parents on the same page. Scheduling time to discuss costs can help both parents anticipate changes and plan for extras that truly make a difference. Plan check-ins at the beginning of each season as usually expenses and patterns change about the same time. This proactive approach helps build mutual understanding and sets the stage for raising kids with less financial friction, highlighting how regular, open communication is the foundation of effective co-parenting.

Madison and José

Let's check in on Madison and José and see how they're managing back-to-school shopping for their two kids, ages 14 and 9, as they work together to create a co-parenting plan that works for both of them.

THE GOOD, THE BAD, AND THE UGLY OF BACK-TO-SCHOOL ROUTINES

"It can't be back-to-school time already!" says Madison. As the saying goes, days are long, but years are short. She can't believe she has a daughter starting high school. Bella is 14 now and into all things fashion and friends. Alex is going into his last year of elementary school and is spending the summer at basketball camp. They both have had a growth spurt. It's time to get ready to go back to school and time to have the conversation with José on how to share the expenses. There are haircuts, school supplies, new sneakers needed, and outfits that fit. The thought of this conversation stresses Madison out. She is now remarried to Bobby, who has two kids of his own. Juggling a blended family can be a challenge especially with a different mindset about financially supporting children. In years past, José overspends when out shopping with the kids right before school starts, in Madison's opinion, and then asks for 50% of the expenses, which upsets Bobby as it affects the number of hours Madison needs to work that month to cover the additional funds. In the past, Madison has not spoken up or refused to pay the unexpected expense as she wants the best for her kids. This year, in July, she decided to be proactive and has asked José to work through the Money Mindset Method to come up with a solution they can

Raising Together, Apart

both emotionally and financially afford. (See Script 12: The Great Back-to-School Budget Debate)

GOAL OR GOALS?

Sophia and William

Stella is a star soccer player for her age, 15. She has been asked to play on a prestigious competitive travel soccer team in the area. William believes it would be a wonderful opportunity for her that could lead to a college scholarship, while Sophia doesn't feel the same way. It wasn't just the money Sophia was concerned about with the new club, it's Stella's time away from friends, school, time to study, and so on that was keeping her up at night—a financial drain for her and a time drain for Stella with all the practices and travel. When Sophia and William got divorced two years earlier they agreed to 50/50 custody. One week on, one week off, and to keep Stella in soccer with a split of 70% from William and 30% Sophia for expenses. While this seemed fair at the time for local rec soccer, it is now starting to look a lot different. William keeps dropping hints to Stella that it is her mom who is against her joining the team, causing tension with the two of them. Every day Stella has been begging her parents for an answer, the coach as well, so it was time for Sophia and William to make the final decision. William suggests they meet and use the Money Mindset Method to find the best solution.

M = Make conversations comfortable

O = One by one

N = Nurture shared goals

E = Evaluate practical solutions

Y = Yes to compassion

CONVERSATIONS WITH YOUR FINANCIAL THERAPIST

Madison and José	Sophia and William
It's the middle of the summer and staying light later so after work they decided to talk at the picnic tables at the park while Alex played basketball. Madison brought a notebook with her, but left her new husband at home. This was a conversation between her and José only.	Due to the quick turnaround on time that the coach needs an answer and work travel for William, they have decided to have a Zoom call to walk through this decision. They set some ground rules before they started the conversations: • Limit distractions. • Put phones in another room. • Set a timer for 30 minutes. • Only talk about soccer. • No one else is allowed in the room. • Stella can't be sneaking around.

M = Make conversations comfortable

O = One by one

N = Nurture shared goals

E = Evaluate practical solutions

Y = Yes to compassion

Inside Madison's book was a detailed list of expenses from last year that she had printed out. As part of her budgeting routine, she keeps the kid's expenses listed in an Excel spreadsheet. It was easy to access the information and help with financial planning year to year.

José shows up feeling like he was going to the principal's office. Madison always rules the family finances with a tight fist. Now he is "free" to make his own decisions and he enjoys buying his kids nice things.

The friction was that "per the divorce decree" all kid expenses were split 50/50, which meant that José was seen as the hero buying the nice things, and on the back end asking Madison for the money she didn't plan for, but didn't want to say no or have her kids return the items they were excited about.

Raising Together, Apart

Madison and José	Sophia and William
Madison wonders: • How much is this going to cost me? • How much time am I going to have to take off work again? • What am I going to do when José overspends? • Bella is starting high school and needs a new haircut and clothes. I want her to feel good about herself. • Shopping with Bella always leaves me feeling so "uncool" and exhausted. José wonders: • Cool; back-to-school time. • When does school start? • Do kids still take lunch boxes? • When can I have them? Let's have some fun. • Who will complete the soccer forms for the school team? I don't want to forget that.	They knew the Money Mindset rules to keep to one question at a time, but one question to answer came with a lot other questions for Sophia: • How will Stella get to practice 30 minutes away every day by 5 p.m.? • When will she get her homework done if practice is four days a week plus travel on the weekends? • How will she get to all the games? Most are overnight trips that will cost money for gas, hotel, a few plane tickets, meals, and so on. William wonders: • What if Stella doesn't like it? • Can she practice enough to improve to be a star on the team? • What if I can't take her to an away tournament because of a work trip?
Topic: They want to decided how to provide for the kids back-to-school expenses within an agreed-on spending amount that they both keep to.	**Topic:** Should Stella play for the travel soccer team and could both of her parents support her to do this both with their time and money?

Sophia reminded William that at any point this conversation wasn't productive to use their code word of *palm tree* that they used to use for money conversations in the past. This will be give them an opportunity to pause and reset after they have time to take a few breaths before re-engaging.

M = Make conversations comfortable

O = One by one

N = Nurture shared goals

E = Evaluate practical solutions

Y = Yes to compassion

CONVERSATIONS WITH YOUR FINANCIAL THERAPIST

This chapter is about co-parenting; therefore, the default shared goal is kid focused. You two might not see eye-to-eye, but there should be at least one piece of common ground. Focus on working through the best solution for your child(ren). This might involve checking your personal feelings aside to do what is best for your family.

Madison and José	Sophia and William
They both want the following: • Both kids need a haircut. • Both kids need to go to the doctor for a wellness visit (no money needed, but time off work). • New sneakers are a must (you don't want to smell Alex's!). • Alex will need new uniforms for school. • Bella is starting high school and for the first time doesn't need to wear a uniform. She is going to need new clothes that are appropriate for school. • Alex can use his backpack from last year, but Bella needs a new one. • Teacher's list for Alex's classroom is long. • Bella will have to buy school supplies, but won't know what she needs until after school starts. Now that they have agreed on what is needed, next up is how to share the time it will take to do the errands, the dollar amount it will take, and the amount of patience needed to take a teenage girl shopping.	They could agree on the following: • Stella loved playing soccer. • The new coach had a great reputation. • Having her stay active in a sport was good for her socially and physically. • Both parents want to be there to support her.

Tip: Place a picture of your kids on the table in front of you. See what and why you are having this conversation.

Raising Together, Apart

M = Make conversations comfortable

O = One by one

N = Nurture shared goals

E = Evaluate practical solutions

Y = Yes to compassion

With two parents (or more), conflict could happen at this stage if you do not allow yourself to be open up to new ideas and solutions. Before starting to brainstorm solutions, take a minute to open up your hearts, your ears, and be open to a possible solution even if it isn't your idea.

Madison and José	Sophia and William
Madison pulls out her Excel spreadsheet and starts to take notes. Looking at last year, they each spent $700. She has allotted $500 this year based on her current work schedule; this is what she can afford, and she shares that information with José.	Sophia spoke with another parent who has a child on the team, and shared that it costs them all-in with a strength conditioning coach, team expenses, dinners on the go due to practice times, and location, hotels, travel fees, and so on $3,500 for the season.
José is still living at home with his mom and has more discretionary money available. He hasn't thought about how much he spends on his kids; he just buys what makes them happy.	That was a big shift from their local soccer team, which was $700 for the year. How will this play out for away travel games? Shared hotel rooms?
They brainstorm six options: 1. Alex has fewer expenses than Bella; Madison can be responsible for all of Alex's expenses and José can be responsible for all of Bella's expenses. 2. They each are mindful of spending. Madison will take all expenses and they will split it 50/50, not to exceed $1,000 total for both kids.	Now it was time to see how they could agree on a way to have Stella play and get her school work done, and financially afford the additional expenses and time the new team will be for both parents. They consider six options: 1. Was there anyone locally they could carpool with or older kids on the team Stella could get a ride from?

CONVERSATIONS WITH YOUR FINANCIAL THERAPIST

Madison and José	Sophia and William
3. "Per the divorce decree" they split all back-to-school expenses, which don't have a limit on them. Sorry, Madison: deal with it.	2. Could she take a study hall period or an athletic schedule to leave early to allow time for studying? William's son had done this and it was helpful. The only downside is the bus can't take her home. She will have to walk. Sophia's house is closer. Does that mean she always walks home to Sophia's during the school week?
4. Divide and conquer: Madison takes the time off work to take the kids to the doctor and hair appointments and pay for those expenses along with school supply shopping. José will take and pay for back-to-school shopping including new sneakers for both kids.	
5. Continue to do what they did last year, spend as needed no matter who has the kids, and split it at the end, whatever the total is.	3. When traveling, instead of staying in the team hotel with two rooms, they could get an Airbnb with more space and share the expense; otherwise, only one parent would go depending on the weekend. Ideally they will alternate trips to keep costs even.
6. Madison keeps track on the spreadsheet of what they both spend, agreeing ahead of time that over her $500 contribution that José will be responsible for the rest 100% on his own.	4. Brainstorm what expenses they could reduce to shift the money into this area for Stella. Reduce money into the college fund to use now as this team could lead to a scholarship?
	5. William recently got a bonus at work that could cover all the expenses. He can pay for it all and expect nothing from Sophia. (Nothing in life is free though, she knows, and this will come with bad-mouthing her to Stella, ugh!)
	6. Per the divorce decree it's a 70/30 split: • $2,450 for William and $1,050 for Sophia • With 50/50 time sharing it won't be easy to split as time to travel to practice, weekends away, expenses, and so on, and Sophia will probably end up spending more than 30% of the costs.

Fact: The National Retail Federation says a typical American household spent over $850 on back-to-school shopping in 2023.

The costs may be significantly different depending on the age of the child and their studies, whether it is elementary or middle school, high school, or college. Here's how it breaks down with average costs:

- Elementary school—$500: At this level, most expenditures are on primary-need items such as school stationery and trousers/skirts. Electronics still needs to be considered a big player.
- Middle school—$600: It is a time when kids require more individual supplies and their first worthwhile electronics, such as tablets. Besides, they begin to be more conscious of the clothes they wear.
- High school—$800: This is where electronics, such as laptops and graphing calculators, get going. Sports, clubs, and cool outfits add more pressure.
- College—$1,200: College students are one of the best markets for buying everything from laptops to textbooks, which are incredibly overpriced, as well as dorm merchandise and clothing for internships and conferences.[1]

Tip: If the child or children are being pulled into the conversation by one parent, it's helpful to then involve the child in the conversation by asking them how they feel about it when *x* parent pulls them into these adult conversations or what do they think we should do (depending on age). It will give you a chance to understand how they feel and also allow them to be heard about the situation. Depending on the age they also might have ideas worth brainstorming.

Sophia is struggling with William, who talks negatively about her to their daughter leading up to their Zoom meeting. She sat down with Stella and had an adult-like conversation with her about what was going on

CONVERSATIONS WITH YOUR FINANCIAL THERAPIST

regarding the topic of the travel soccer team. Sophia shared with her the concerns, fears, worries, and financial pains she will experience if they go to the new team. Stella listened and shared with her mom why it was so important to her to join the new team and made a promise to work hard on and off the field to make them both proud. (See Script 13: Time for a Family Huddle.)

M = Make conversations comfortable

O = One by one

N = Nurture shared goals

E = Evaluate practical solutions

Y = Yes to compassion

You are doing it. You are having the uncomfortable conversation. Remember to be kind to yourself and those around you.

Madison and José	Sophia and William
José is annoyed that he has to be mindful of spending on his kids, but he's also aware that his business has had a few bad years in the past and that could be him next year. He shows empathy here to Madison, which will go a long way in their co-parenting together. Madison is feeling grateful that José is willing to have a talk and try something new this year. Communication as to why there is a need to shift the spending or splitting of costs is key to understanding, problem-solving, and mutual respect, which the kids will notice. Driving home, Madison smiles, drops her shoulders, and exhales.	After the conversation with Stella, Sophia was proud of herself and poured herself a cold beverage to toast with. She was going to make this work. William went down to the hotel gym after the Zoom and had a great workout knowing he was advocating for Stella and now she will be on the team. When the timer went off, William thanked Sophia for taking the time to make this a joint decision for their child versus him just signing her up and having her "deal with it." They can handle the upcoming season as a team of three. It wasn't easy to do, but it will make the season go a lot smoother for all of them working together than against one another.

Where Are They Now?

Madison and José are attending the back-at-school meeting for Bella and admiring how well they adjusted to this year's back-to-school stressful time, especially with their other "baby" starting high school. While it looked different this year than in years past, due to the kids' needs/wants and rising cost of things, with solid communication both the kids and parents started the school year off feeling ready for success instead of stressed.

Here are their three options:

1. Madison is responsible for Alex's needs and José for Bella's.
2. José picks up the entire bill.
3. Madison takes the time off work for doctor appointments, schedule pick-ups, and school supply shopping, and José pays for back-to-school clothes and sneakers.

What Would You Do?

Madison enjoyed her time with Alex, getting him ready for school. It is so nice to get one-on-one time with a child and not take a teenager shopping (😂). She also knew it was important for her to be the one who takes the kids to their doctor appointments, as she hasn't missed a year and this wasn't going to be the year. They decided to combine options 1 and 3, which worked out well for the entire family.

Where Are They Now?

The coach was ecstatic to hear that Stella was joining the team. Her fierceness and skill were the missing pieces they needed to make it to nationals this year.

At the end of their Zoom conversation, Sophia and William narrowed it down to three options. They agreed to sleep on it and text at 9 a.m. with what option they each wanted to go with. If they agreed, the issue was resolved; if they didn't, they would then hop onto a call to work out another solution.

1. William pays for all fees and additional training with his bonus. General travel will be paid for by the parent responsible for that week. They both will be responsible for their own hotel rooms and pay 50% of the room Stella stays in.
2. Stella enrolls in the athletic schedule, leaving school early each day to have extra time for training and homework. She walks home to Sophia's house each day where Sophia's friend's daughter takes her to practice at 4:15 every afternoon. Expenses are split 70/30 for fees/training, while travel is covered by the parent who is listed as primary that weekend (unless plane tickets are involved—70/30 split for those). (See Script 14: The Game Within the Game: Tournament Logistics.)
3. Sophia informs Stella that she is responsible for the additional expenses for the team. When she isn't with her team, Stella offers training workouts for kids 3–8 years old and all the money that she makes goes into a travel soccer fund.

What Would You Do?

Sitting on the plane in a row of three, William, Stella, and Sophia are ready for take-off. It's the end of the season and they are headed into the national championships in North Carolina. It has been an exciting season with ups and downs both physically and emotionally. Sophia and William are happy with their joint decision to go with option 2. Sophia got to see her daughter every day (bonus!) and Stella was able to join the team of her dreams.

Raising Together, Apart

MONEY MANTRA

I am wealthy, focused, and empowered.
I am and have enough.
I trust my decisions and honor my growth.
Every step I take builds freedom, abundance, and peace.

XOXO, Your Future Self

DO YOU BELIEVE ADULT CHILDREN SHOULD SUPPORT THEIR PARENTS FINANCIALLY?

SOURCE: LET'S TALK FINANCES CONVERSATION CARDS

CHAPTER EIGHT

ROLE REVERSAL

NAVIGATING FINANCES WITH AGING PARENTS

CONVERSATIONS WITH YOUR FINANCIAL THERAPIST

This chapter features Averi and her mom, Natalie, and Gabe with his parents, Ernie and Mary.

Averi's mom, Natalie, has been living alone for the past several years since Averi's dad passed away. Averi has started to notice that her mom has been repeating herself lately and forgetting to do simple tasks.

Gabe is home for the holidays and his parents, Ernie and Mary, are ready to share their "when I die" folder with him since all of their friends these days seem to be passing away. Because Gabe is an only child, they don't want him to be overwhelmed when the time comes or feeling confused on what to do next.

Script 15: Preparing for the Last Mile

Script 16: Passing on Peace: The Legacy Conversation

Script 17: Sibling Solution: Navigating Mom's Next Chapter

Financial insecurity in senior citizens is a growing trend. Almost half the US population ages 55–66 have no retirement savings, and women tend to have even less than men.[1] What does that mean to their families? What would this mean for yours? The lack of savings has led to parents turning into dependents of their children with everything from moving in with them, to having their cell phone and medical bills paid for, and the adult children becoming their caregivers. While in some cultures this is expected, in others it is out of guilt or feeling that there is no other solution.

This can have an impact on your own financial goals for retirement, thus creating a cycle of lack of planning for retirement that may trickle down to your kids. Talking about money is challenging at all stages of life especially if you grew up in a home where money was not talked about. Bringing up this topic with your parent(s) can feel awkward or uncomfortable, like the first time they tried to talk about sex with you. If you are reading this and saying, "We never had the sex talk," chances are you haven't had a financial talk either with them. This chapter will guide you through several ways to approach the topic.

The roller coaster of parenting starts out with something nice like "Mommy, you are so pretty"; this was what my toddler daughters used to say to me when I would get dressed to head out the door. Then, came the teenage years of "You are wearing *that* out of the house?" One day, they will show up at my nursing home and help me to get dressed.

Our perspectives and relationships will change over time with ourselves and with family members. Navigating the transition from childhood to adulthood with your parents also comes with twists and turns for the roller coaster of life. One minute your parents are your shiny heroes and the next minute you are showing them how to reset their password for their online bank account for the tenth time. For some it will come unexpectedly and drastically due to a sudden illness, and for others it will be a slow transition. Either way you get there it can be tricky to navigate when the adult children step in to support aging parents physically, emotionally, and potentially financially.

IS AGE JUST A NUMBER?

For me, when I think of an "old person" I find myself thinking about my great aunt sitting in a nursing home in her late eighties, cruising around on her scooter to get to meals and art classes, with her flip phone that she never could figure out sitting on the counter. One perk I think she enjoyed having the most was selective hearing. She would share stories with us kids, but when she didn't feel like talking she would tell her dinner partners that the hearing aid battery was dead and she would enjoy her meal in silence. This made me laugh. Aging also can have some perks :).

CONVERSATIONS WITH YOUR FINANCIAL THERAPIST

What I didn't see as a kid was the slow decline that got her to where she was. By the time she moved to Florida she was already old and, in my eyes, ready for the nursing home.

Aging is really a lot of small losses over time. Let's use going out to dinner as an example. First it starts with small things such as in your forties with your eyesight, you need reading glasses and are using the flashlight on your phone to read the menu. Next, you are asking people to turn the music down and requesting to go to a different restaurant because it is too noisy inside. Then the day comes when you understand why older people eat dinner at 4:30 p.m. when driving at night becomes too hard to navigate.

The same also happens on the financial side of their lives. Simple tasks like paying monthly bills that have been routine for years may start to be a challenge for aging parents. This can be a variety of reasons, such as emergency hospital stay, poor eyesight to read the correct amounts on bills, arthritis that makes writing checks more challenging, lack of mobility to get to the bank, walking to the mailbox or forgetting to check emails as frequently, and overall memory loss issues, to name a few. At the same time there could be shame in their financial situation that they wish not to share or burden you with. It is not uncommon for elders to be vulnerable to financial scams, insufficient funds for retirement, and/or confusion on paperwork, wills, and estate plans; instead of asking their child for help, they keep quiet.

Averi

Averi has a growing concern for her Mom, Natalie. Recently she has noticed when she calls that her mom is repeating herself and forgetting simple things like dinner recipes she has made thousands of times. On a recent visit home Averi went to her doctor's appointment with Natalie where they discussed the progression of her early onset Alzheimer's. It was in that doctor's appointment that Averi learned that they had a family history of Alzheimer's. This was new information for Averi. Her mom forgot to share that information with her. What else did she not know about her mom's history?

Role Reversal

After leaving the doctor's appointment Averi knew it was time to have some very hard and honest conversations with her mom to learn all she could before her mom was no longer able to share this information. Which brought up another concern: what is her mom's full financial picture? She knew from past conversations that her mom was living off a small pension and Social Security. She had lost most of her savings in a dating scam (more on that next). She could financially support herself today with the modest lifestyle she has, but what about future memory care if it is needed? Does Natalie have long-term health care? Averi doubted it, which led to a lot more questions in her head on the drive home—who will take care of her mom both physically and financially in the not so far off future? (See Script 15: Preparing for the Last Mile.)

A few years back, after being a widow for a year, Natalie decided to try online dating. It sounded like a good idea at the time. She was feeling lonely, but what happened next no one was prepared for. Natalie was love bombed (definition: an instance of lavishing someone with attention or affection, especially in order to influence or manipulate them[2]). Over the next several months Natalie was feeling loved, cared for, and happy with her new younger boyfriend who worked overseas. She had feelings she hadn't felt in a long time. He would call and text her all day long, be interested in her stories about her day, and dream of them sipping cocktails by the pool on the soon-to-come vacation. She was in the "rose-colored glasses" phase of the relationship. But she didn't share with her family a lot of the details about her dating life—it just felt weird to do that. In the course of less than six months, her "boyfriend" managed to scam her out of $50,000. By the time her family got involved it was already too late: her savings account was wiped out.

To the reader this might sound crazy, but to an older woman looking for attention it can happen very easily. This isn't a women-only issue either. I recently had a client spend all of his savings over four years on an overseas relationship with a person he never met in person. He is now 63 with no savings.

IT'S ROLE REVERSAL TIME

US seniors lose $28.3 billion annually as a result of financial exploitation, according to an AARP study.[3] Financial elder abuse is a real thing and happens daily. It is when someone steals money or possessions of value from an older person. I have seen older women living on Social Security to very powerful successful people in older years be taken advantage of with their finances. It has shocked me over the years to see how and whom this affects. Don't think it won't happen to your or my family. You might be surprised. The roller coaster of life happens to us all and sometimes it involves this dip and twist.

Four signs of financial elder abuse to look out for:

- Unusual activity in a person's bank accounts, including large, frequent, or unexplained withdrawals
- ATM withdrawals by an older person who has never used a debit or ATM card
- Withdrawals from bank accounts or transfers between accounts your loved one cannot explain
- Requests for gift cards to be sent to friends you haven't met before

* * *

Ernie, Mary, and Gabe

Ernie and Mary, Gabe's parents, are having a hard time adjusting to senior living although they just moved into an over-55 community and love all the activities. But seeing their family and friends start to get sick and some of them dying has been difficult on them, especially Ernie who always felt like he would live forever. His brother passed away of a heart attack earlier this year and his finances were not in order for his family, which has caused a lot of extra delays with court dates, fees for attorneys, and conflicts with family members on how to handle the estate. Ernie has promised himself he will not do that to his family. Gabe has been called in to have a meeting

Role Reversal

with his parents to learn more about their financial situation. (See Script 16: Passing on Peace: The Legacy Conversation.) On a recent trip home, Gabe walked into the kitchen and saw papers all over the table and felt a tightness in his chest. He was not prepared for this conversation. His dad was his rock; how was he going to help the guy who knows everything? Was he really the best person for the job? He spent the first few days home avoiding being alone with his dad to avoid having that adult sit-down talk, until one morning over coffee Gabe gave himself a pep talk as he recalled using the Money Mindset Method to help him through other financial conversations. He called for his dad to join him in the kitchen.

If you or your parent(s) are ready to address finances here's 10 actions to start:

1. Start the conversations early and have it as often as possible.
   - Monthly meetings to go over expenses, upcoming events like surgeries, planning family vacations, reviewing taxes, medical bills, and so on.
   - Create a calendar invite for both you and your parents to stay focused.

2. Ask them to share a list of professionals they use, from the plumber, to the vet, to an estate attorney, to a financial advisor.
   - A shared Google Doc is a good place to store this information, especially if you live far away. Or, if your parents prefer a written list, know where the list is located.

3. Start gradual to build trust.
   - Sharing their life information will take time, so be patient and start with smaller topics/bills that won't upset them.
   - Build trust and confidence over time to allow for harder conversations later on.

CONVERSATIONS WITH YOUR FINANCIAL THERAPIST

4. Simplify bills.
   ○ Automate, consolidate, and if needed take over responsibility for payments.

5. Monitor for changes in patterns of purchases.
   ○ ATM or credit card charges are increased.
   ○ There are unexpected investment withdraws.

6. Take an inventory of financial and legal documents.
   ○ Review documents they currently have (bank statements, pensions, life insurance policies, investment accounts, will, trust/estate documents).
   ○ Make sure the power of attorney is updated, along with health care surrogates, which will allow you to talk to doctors or financial professionals on their behalf.
   ○ Identify any documents that are missing and whom to contact to create them.

7. Update contact information on financial and legal documents.
   ○ Beneficiaries might have passed away or moved residences since the last time it was updated.

8. Know where the documents are.
   ○ Agree on a shared place to keep the important documents.

9. Do not commingle finances.
   ○ Keep your finances separate.

10. Communicate and document your actions.
   ○ This will help build trust with your parents and siblings.

Let's peek in to see how Averi and Gabe are going to handle the uncomfortable conversations about learning about their parent's

Role Reversal

financial situation. They both have decided to use the Money Mindset Method to provide structure to the conversation and decision-making that might be needed for their aging parents.

M = Make conversations comfortable

O = One by one

N = Nurture shared goals

E = Evaluate practical solutions

Y = Yes to compassion

Averi	Gabe
Averi asks to meet with her mom to talk through a few long-term concerns she has regarding her finances and health. They choose to have the meeting in her mom's home office after lunch that day. Natalie was uneasy about the meeting, but she also knew it was a needed conversation. By having it in Natalie's office Averi thought it would make her mom feel more comfortable and if needed her documents could be nearby.	Gabe wasn't comfortable having this conversation no matter when it would happen. He was not prepared to be an adult in this situation. After several days at home, seeing the papers laying around, and having a few small conversations with his parents while out walking, he was feeling a little more relaxed. The kitchen table was always the place they had family conversations, so before the day got busy Gabe and his parents began to sort the documents.

M = Make conversations comfortable

O = One by one

N = Nurture shared goals

E = Evaluate practical solutions

Y = Yes to compassion

CONVERSATIONS WITH YOUR FINANCIAL THERAPIST

Averi	Gabe
This was going to be the first of many needed conversations. Averi has a lot of questions that she wants answers to, but she knows that she can't get anywhere by overwhelming her mom in the first meeting.	Just sitting down, Gabe is already feeling stressed. There are papers everywhere, his dad is talking in circles, and his mom is nervously pacing nearby.
Here are the first questions that came to her mind: • What documents need to be in place for power of attorney for financial and medical decision-making? • Does Natalie have a living will? • Is her will/estate plan updated and where is it? • What is Natalie's financial situation? • Who manages Natalie's money? • Where is the mortgage with? • Does Natalie have an estate attorney? • Who's her accountant and where are her past taxes? • What does she want Averi to do for help? • How does Natalie want to capture her memories? • When will Natalie stop driving? • What are her monthly expenses? • Can Natalie add Averi to her accounts? Way too many questions to tackle at one time.	Gabe has asked if they can stick to one thing at a time and then asks his dad, "Where do you want to start? And what is the goal of this meeting?" Ernie came back with, "Let's start with the life insurance policy. Who the policy is with and what I want you or your mother to use it for."
Topic: Today they will focus on gathering the information Natalie has already.	**Topic:** This meeting is to leave Gabe in better shape than Ernie's brother left him being the executor of his estate. Ernie wants Gabe to know every detail of his and Mary's financial and legal lives. Ernie has gathered all the necessary information, and gestures to hundreds of papers around the table.

Role Reversal

M = Make conversations comfortable

O = One by one

N = **Nurture shared goals**

E = Evaluate practical solutions

Y = Yes to compassion

Averi	Gabe
Today's goal is to gather the basics of who is on "Team Natalie": • Doctor names • Accountant • Mortgage • Lawyer Establish a place to keep online in a secure folder and in Natalie's office for the paper files. Schedule weekly meetings for the next six weeks to continue conversations.	The understanding that Ernie wants his only child to know the ins and out of his finances is something they can agree on. Never being in this role with his father, Gabe is uncomfortable asking questions and knowing his parents' worth. He was surprised to learn that they are not in as good shape as he thought they would be.

M = Make conversations comfortable

O = One by one

N = Nurture shared goals

E = **Evaluate practical solutions**

Y = Yes to compassion

Averi	Gabe
Create a list of professionals. Research apps that can keep information that is secure and shareable. Averi's coworker recently mentioned an app she was using. Make a note to text her.	The life insurance policy was the most important information his dad wanted to share as Ernie felt it was the gift he could give his family after he was gone.

CONVERSATIONS WITH YOUR FINANCIAL THERAPIST

Averi	Gabe
Averi needs to figure out how she can spend more time at her mom's house to help cook meals and go to doctor appointments in the next 12 months. • Natalie can still cook as long as she sets timers to remember to take the food off the stove. It only happened once that she had burned dinner, but they both know it won't be the last. • Averi set up an Alexa alert for 7 p.m. each night to remind her mom to turn off all electronics. • Work was going to be a challenge to take off for each appointment. Averi set aside one day each month for doctor's appointments. Now the goal is to schedule any appointments on those days to limit the interruptions each week. She also reached out to her mom's cousin to see if she could be available as a backup for appointments. It was important to her that someone else was there to help remember what the doctors said and/or report on how her mom was really doing. Her cousin agreed. • Averi needs to reach out to her brother to see how he can or will support his mother. He hasn't been involved with the family much, but at the same time—she's his mom, too.	Ernie gave Gabe a copy of the policy and shared with the family on how he wanted them to use the $250,000 policy for in-home health care for his wife, travel if she was well enough to do it, and money for Gabe's some-day wedding. The problem was the agent listed on the policy had died a few years earlier. Ernie noted that and called the company to set up a meeting for the family to meet the new agent.

M = Make conversations comfortable

O = One by one

N = Nurture shared goals

E = Evaluate practical solutions

Y = Yes to compassion

Role Reversal

Averi	Gabe
Averi can sense her mom's nervousness about the next phase of life. She is aware when speaking to her to use patience and deep breathing (on occasion). While Natalie is frustrated with her situation she is grateful for Averi's time and attention. Natalie often finds herself going through old pictures and making videos of her memories for Averi to find one day as a thank-you.	Gabe left that visit home feeling better than he thought he would. The kitchen table meeting ended up lasting three hours. A lot of information was shared, more questions came up, and they all agreed to do this again next month. Gabe now understands his dad is trying to help him, not overwhelm him when the time comes that he passes. After the meeting, he hugged his dad tight and thanked him. The information he learned might not be what he expected (like the second mortgage on the house), but at least now he had a road map for that dreadful day.

Where Are They Now?

It's been two years and Natalie is getting lost more often when doing routine errands around town. She is often late to appointments and finds it harder to live on her own. Averi has been promoted at work, working 80 hours a week, and trying to manage her mother's care while trying not to get frustrated at her mother, not an easy task. The time has come to look for a new living situation for Natalie with more oversight.

Here are their options:

1. Go to a full-time memory care facility an hour away from Averi's office, but her mother doesn't have the funds to live there longer than one year. Her overall health is good, which means she could live a long time. It will cost Averi out of pocket $8,000/month (or call her brother, whom she hasn't talked to, and ask for support).

2. Take away Natalie's car, and hire help during the day in her current home. This won't cost much extra, but it will isolate her from socializing and getting to appointments.
3. Find an assisted living facility with a step-up area for memory care. Natalie can pay for three years and after that Averi will have to pay out-of-pocket.

What Would You Do?

After visiting a few assisted living facilities, consulting with an elder care advocate, and talking to doctors and staff at her recent appointments, Averi made the decision to move her mom into an assisted facility that has a step-up memory care unit on the same property. The one she picked costs a little more but is closer to her home, which will allow for her to drop by before or after work relieving some of her guilt. Her brother has agreed to take a week off work and be in charge of the move along with sending $500/month to cover some of the fees. (See Script 17: Sibling Solution: Navigating Mom's Next Chapter.)

This is a good reminder that your financial goals are important, too. If you are going to be supporting your family financially, before you make commitments, review your own finances. What you want to give versus what you can give might look different. Create boundaries on what you are willing to do with your money and time. For example, I can give $3,000 and two weekends of my time a year. Together with other siblings, family members, or friends, develop a long-term plan on how to support your parents' needs while not depleting your financial goals.

Where Are They Now?

This time it is just Gabe and his mother Mary sitting at the kitchen table. Ernie passed away earlier that year from pancreatic cancer. This time it was

Role Reversal

Gabe's turn to help educate and comfort his mom on the topic of money. In their traditional marriage, Ernie did all the finances and Mary was aware but not involved. Mary knew intellectually that she had to pay the electric bill each month, file taxes every year in April, and the name of the account, but that is where her understanding ended. She did not know how or where to start to take ownership with family finances.

Here are their options:

1. Gabe took over all the family finances and put allowance money into his mother's checking account each month.
2. Mary took over the everyday bills and left the investments and taxes to Gabe to manage with the professionals.
3. Mary felt controlled her whole life by men with money and took the power back by managing all the finances.

What Option Would You Choose?

Gabe and Mary went with option 2. After a few months of working together, Mary felt comfortable managing the finances for day-to-day activities. She would consult with Gabe on larger financial decisions and ask him to attend any meeting with an advisor or attorneys with her. They keep monthly meetings and arrange to have Mary's will and power of attorney updated to reflect the new changes.

Resources: if you need support with aging family members:

National Institute on Aging (https://www.nia.nih.gov/)

National Alliance for Caregiving (https://www.caregiving.org/)

MONEY MANTRA

I am wealthy, focused, and empowered.
I am and have enough.
I trust my decisions and honor my growth.
Every step I take builds freedom, abundance, and peace.

XOXO, Your Future Self

**WHAT IS ONE
FINANCIAL SECRET
YOU HAVE?**

**IS IT HINDERING
OR
HELPING YOU?**

SOURCE: LET'S TALK FINANCES CONVERSATION CARDS

CHAPTER NINE

LAST WISHES AND LOOSE ENDS

ESTATE PLANNING REALITIES

CONVERSATIONS WITH YOUR FINANCIAL THERAPIST

This chapter features José and Sam.

José had cared for his mother, Marta, and her home for years, treating both with great care and respect. Before her passing, she assured him the house would be his, but without anything in writing, his siblings aren't on board. Now, as emotions run high, José must navigate grief, family tension, and financial uncertainty while trying to honor his mother's wishes and find a way forward with his family.

Sam's world was turned upside down after losing her father, Sal, to a short battle with cancer. For 54 years, her parents shared a traditional marriage where Sal handled all financial matters, leaving her mother with little knowledge of their finances. In his final days, Sal mentioned only that "the paperwork is above the TV," offering no further details. Now, as her grieving mother struggles to piece together their financial situation, Sam steps in to help. Together, they must navigate unfamiliar territory, uncovering accounts, bills, and plans, all while managing the emotional weight of their loss.

Script 18: Sibling Group Chat
Script 19: But Where Will I Live?
Script 20: Balance Sheets and Inner Peace

Our relationship with money is one that stays with us until the day we die. Actually, it lingers a lot longer than that, as our loved ones handle the estate planning or lack thereof. Our relationship with money can have a big impact on those around us after our death depending on how well or how poorly you have legally and financially planned. One thing I can promise you: we will all die. What I can't promise you is that you will know when that will happen and how much will be in the bank. For most of us, there will be several open bank accounts, credit cards, mortgages, deeds to cars

Last Wishes and Loose Ends

and houses, and insurance policies to sort out, regardless if you take charge of your estate planning or leave it to your heirs to figure out. The time of death can be for some in their early twenties from a car accident to natural death at the age of 103. What I have learned from my clients is that it is never too early to plan for the unexpected. If you don't, you are leaving it up to others to make assumptions (and we know what that means), you'll pay additional fees to the court and lawyers for probate, and possibly worse, you'll find yourself digging through drawers to find important documents and everything else you stuffed away years ago. You are also leaving the decision-making up to the laws of your state to determine who receives your assets, who administers your estate, and who becomes the guardian of any minor children, decisions that might not align with your best interests or values.

NEVER TOO EARLY TO START YOUR ESTATE PLAN

In fact, anyone over the age of 18 should have some minimal estate planning documents in place. I was surprised by this initially. But as I saw kids go off to college, get into accidents, have an unexpected hospital visit, and their parents do not have access to medical information, I realized why this was so important to have in place. Some universities have it now as part of their initial paperwork during orientation, other families find support with their local attorney, or people use online apps to create power of attorney for health and finances, Health Insurance Portability and Accountability Act releases, and Family Educational Rights and Privacy Act waivers. This can cost between $80 and $500.

> **PROMPT**
>
> Let me ask you a few questions first:
> - Do you have a will?_____
> - How about an estate plan?_____
> - When was the last time you reviewed or updated it?_____
> - Who knows where those documents are stored? _____

It may or may not surprise you to learn that 50% of people do not have a will and only 30% have estate plans. What does that mean if you do not have plans in place at the time of death? Let's break it down. After you die, if you do not have an adequate estate plan in place, your property, bank accounts, car titles, and so on—generally all your belongings—will go through probate before anyone can sell anything on your behalf. As a result, this often creates a delay in settling your estate, which could be weeks, months, or years and cost your estate money in court fees and legal expenses and time for your loved ones. There is such a backlog in the courts that you cannot sell the properties of the estate (home, cars, etc.) until it is settled, which could mean additional expenses with costs of your property such as mortgage, utilities, insurances, taxes, for several months.

Today you can create an estate plan online with various apps or directly with an estate attorney. It varies by state, but generally any estate of $75,000 or more needs to go through probate. Probate is the court process of passing on the decedent's assets to a rightful heir. In 2023 alone there were over three million cases in the United States.[1] Based on information gathered on the estate lawyers and attorneys sector (which includes probate services), it is estimated revenue of roughly $17.8 billion in 2023 alone.[2] Quick math: that is roughly $6,000 per person who passes away if they all went through probate. The old saying, you pay now or you pay later, stands true here.

Estate planning can range from $500 to $7,000 or more depending on how complex the estate. So, why don't more people have an estate plan in place? It often comes down to emotions. Remember the 90/10 split on

Last Wishes and Loose Ends

emotions versus logic on financial decisions? It is no different here when it comes to investing in estate planning. I hear clients say they don't have enough assets to merit one, or others think it would cost too much money to put one in place, and many think it is only for the ultra-rich and/or the entire process is too complicated and it falls off the to-do list of life until it's too late.

PROMPT

The topic of death and dying usually comes with emotions, big emotions. What emotions are showing up now as we talk about estate planning?

For some, having an estate plan in place for their loved ones after death provides a sense of security while for others it brings a sense of fear. Facing mortality and thinking about end-of-life decisions can feel overwhelming and uncomfortable for some. If this is you, you aren't alone. This chapter is designed to help understand the importance of taking the steps to have a plan in place so that your legacy is in a better situation than if you do no estate planning. You don't want the last memories your family and friends have of you to be tarnished by lack of planning on your part. I am sure you can think of a few people who no longer talk to family members over an inheritance dispute. I don't want that to be you!

José

Let's take José for example. He was living at home with his mom since his divorce and, as he is the oldest child, he has been helping his family since they came to this country. Marta, his mother, expected that when she passed away he would figure out the finances, including the deed to the house. When his Mom passed six months ago, she left behind nothing in writing—no will or estate planning documents. She assumed (there's that word again) that her kids would figure it out. Since living with his mother the past five years,

José has not only paid the mortgage but also put a new roof on the home. From what she told him, this is his home and in his mind he plans to live there forever. His two siblings do not see it that way, and want to sell the house because they need the cash. José feels differently and believes the siblings want to sell the house because they are jealous that he is living there and have always felt he was their mother's favorite. Family fights after a loved one passes away is not uncommon: 44% of estate disputes involve siblings.[3]

Greed is rarely the main motive when it comes to family fights. It is often a deeper emotional issue tied to the money in question. Money is often just a way people keep score, leverage control, or show love and approval. Think back to your childhood sibling fights. Rarely was it over who ate the last popsicle, but the buildup of emotions of the things happening before and when the icy treat was disappearing. The same is true with money disputes as adults.

Meanwhile, José is losing sleep, becoming frustrated with all the back-and-forth text messages from his siblings, and decides to hold a family meeting to walk through the best way they as a family can administer their Mother's estate.

GET UNCOMFORTABLE

Estate planning with your kids can be uncomfortable, but what about with your spouse? Death is a sensitive and emotional topic that many people would rather avoid. Discussing it can feel overwhelming or morbid especially if you are in a loving relationship that you want to last forever. Often I hear someone say that they didn't want to bring up the topic as it might stress or worry their spouse unnecessarily. Putting off these conversations might feel good at the moment, but in reality they hurt their partner in the long run when you are no longer there to hold their hand and support them through the unknown. I worked with a client whose husband passed away and her role in their marriage did not include handling the finances, which meant now that she was alone she had to try and figure out what "all this meant." She had gone to dinner with their financial advisor a few times over the years, but that was it. She didn't know the accountant's name, where the bank accounts were, or even if they had life insurance. Now she was left feeling helpless and confused on how to move forward. She isn't alone here. This also happens to Sam's mom.

Sam

Sam is devastated when her dad passes away after a short battle with cancer. He was her rock, her biggest cheerleader, and the person who helped her become financially independent. Her mom comes to her shortly after Sal, Sam's dad, passes and says, "The lawn company knocked on the door asking for payment. I have no idea how to pay them or if they are even our lawn service." Sam knows this was a bigger issue than paying the lawn company. Although her Dad had always taken care of the finances, she had assumed (there's that word again) that her mother was in the know on the financial decisions, especially since Sal had raised Sam to be so financially independent. Apparently, this was not the case. Sam realizes she needs to prioritize helping her mother understand her bills, investments, mortgage, and car loan paperwork—all of it. First Sam has to find Sal's laptop and paperwork above the TV where he told her to look when the time comes. Well, the time has come.

What you discover during this process after the death of a loved one can be shocking both in a good way (hello, windfall of money) or in a bad way (debt you were unaware of). Take a moment to honor that your loved one was probably doing the best they could with the knowledge they had.

If you recall, we get our money mindset from three major areas of our lives: background, religion/culture, and experiences. Handling your loved one's estate is now (or will be) part of your personal experiences. Take notes as you get to decide what you want to take away from this for yourself and your loved ones.

M = Make conversations comfortable

O = One by one

N = Nurture shared goals

E = Evaluate practical solutions

Y = Yes to compassion

The goal here is to create a calm, open space to discuss everyone's feelings, concerns, and ideas without judgment. After a loved one's death emotions can be very high, so it is important to set the tone of the meeting to allow it to be productive. Give thought to the time of day, number of people included, temperature of the room, and the ability for everyone to feel that they have an opportunity to speak. If you're going to be in a large setting with multiple people, one suggestion could be to set a timer to allow everyone two minutes for opening remarks (no responses at this time) or pass the mic allowing one person at a time to talk.

Often this is a time when a lot of new information is shared so it is important to have an environment that is quiet to allow for fewer distractions and lighting that is cozy enough to feel comfortable but bright enough to read all the small print. It's important as well to build in time to take breaks to allow your and everyone else's brain to absorb and recalibrate information throughout the meeting.

José	Sam
José selected a Sunday night to have everyone over for dinner and a conversation. He requested only immediate family members—no spouse, kids, dog, and so on. (See Script 18: Sibling Group Chat.)	Tuesday after work Sam went over to her parents' house. Her mom was there making dinner and wandering around the kitchen feeling a little displaced.

José	Sam
Keeping the conversation to immediate family will help make sure everyone has a chance to speak their own opinion without outside influences.	Sam pulls out dad's computer and looks at her mom for the password—they both shrug their shoulders and laugh, this was going to be a scavenger hunt of an evening. Lucky for them they also knew Sal had a few favorite passwords he liked to use and after two tries they were in.

M = Make conversations comfortable

O = One by one

N = Nurture shared goals

E = Evaluate practical solutions

Y = Yes to compassion

José	Sam
José's focus is to stay in the house, continue paying the mortgage, and keep making updates to the structure. He does not plan to pay out to his siblings any equity in the home as they haven't been part of the upkeep or their mom's care financially.	Sam wants to first see what information they have before she knows what questions to ask or what is missing. Here mom brainstorms questions: • Will I be okay? • Do I have money to live on and how will I do this alone now? • Can I stay in the house? • Do I need to move? I'm not ready to do that. Sam takes her mom's hand and says they will do this together.

CONVERSATIONS WITH YOUR FINANCIAL THERAPIST

José	Sam
His siblings have questions: • How much equity is the house? • How much can we sell it for? • When can I get my money? • Why do you feel you can just live here and take over the house? • You have always been mom's favorite—Why should her saying the house was yours not be a surprise, yet there is nothing in writing. • Wait, we have to pay an attorney for probate? How much is that? Who is going to pay for that?	Sam tells her mom they will first list the questions they have right now: • What are Dad's passwords for computer and cell phone? • Do you know his email password? • Are there bank statements laying around? • Do you have a savings account? • What is the attorney's name for estate planning you did 10 years ago? • Are there any bills due today or past due? Where can we find them? • Where is Dad's wallet? • What do we need to cancel ASAP?
Topic: Figuring out the family home and finances without tearing the family apart after José's mom's passing.	**Topic:** Organizing and uncovering financial and legal information after losing Sam's dad.

Note: All of the fighting and sleepless nights could have been avoided if José's mom had an estate plan clearly expressing her personal wishes to avoid probate. It would have also taken out the guessing for the kids, the finger-pointing, hurt feelings, and attorney costs for probate.

Tip: Write your objective down and put it on a sticky note in front of you to stay focused when engaging in financial conversations.

Last Wishes and Loose Ends

This is a great reminder to add estate planning back on to your life's to-do list today.

M = Make conversations comfortable

O = One by one

N = Nurture shared goals

E = Evaluate practical solutions

Y = Yes to compassion

Closure can look different for each person when dealing with the emotional and financial pieces of a death of a loved one. This is the time to focus on the goals you have in common. It might not be the first issue on your list or theirs but starting on a common goal will help move the conversation in a positive direction because settling an estate can take months to years. Having the common conversations first helps build trust and respect for when the time comes for the tricker conversations.

Tip: Identify three to five messages that are keeping you awake at night with worry. Write them down.

What is the common theme?_____

José	Sam
Focus on fairness, not winning.	Focus on finding out what they do know today versus what they don't. It is easy to get distracted by the unknowns.
Explore comprises. Why do the siblings want money from the estate? Is there a way to obtain their needs in other ways?	For Sam's mom there are several things keeping her up at night. She shares with Sam that the biggest concern is whether she is going to have to move and leave the house they lived in for 30 years. (See Script 19: But Where Will I Live Now?)

CONVERSATIONS WITH YOUR FINANCIAL THERAPIST

José	Sam
Mom did a good job raising the kids. She would be very upset to see them all fighting right now.	
Common goal: To find a fair solution that meets everyone's financial needs while preserving family relationships and honoring their mom's memory.	**Common goal:** Find out what the cost of staying in the home will be for Sam's mom and if she has the income to cover the costs.

M = Make conversations comfortable

O = One by one

N = Nurture shared goals

E = Evaluate practical solutions

Y = Yes to compassion

When working through family disputes, it helps to start by understanding what everyone needs and why they feel they need it the way that they do. Sometimes it's about money, but more often it's more emotional or tied to a sense of fairness. Take time to brainstorm different options and think about what's realistic, keeping in mind the long-term impact versus short-term wins. Look for solutions that align with the shared goal of keeping family relationships strong and respecting everyone's interests. Bringing in a neutral third party, like a mediator or financial therapist, can help keep things fair for everyone involved. Most important, keep the conversation open and be willing to adjust as needed. A little flexibility and understanding can go a long way in finding a solution that works for everyone.

After everyone has a chance to talk and learn more about each other's reasons for wanting the profits of the house, keeping the home in the family, and maintaining a relationship, José and his siblings came up with a few options.

Sam and her mom sit down and unlock Sal's cell phone, take out a notebook and pen, and start to look for clues on what bills he has been paying and where the accounts are located. While Sam looks on the computer,

Last Wishes and Loose Ends

her mom starts to go through the pile of papers that were above the TV. Together they gather the information.

José	Sam
Options: 1. Sell the house and divide the profits equally. (José doesn't like this idea.)	Sam has set aside three hours to gather the information tonight. So far they have found the mortgage payment information, the bank account for bills, the car loan, and house bills are now set up on autopay in the account. They still don't know how much the home owners association fees are and if any additional taxes need to be paid or if it was in an escrow account with the bank.
2. Sell the house, divide the profits after José gets back the money he put in for the mortgage and the new roof, and legal fees are covered for probate.	For now, they know Sam's mom can stay in the house no matter what it takes for at least six months based on the bank accounts they found tonight. Three hours were not enough to learn everything, but they made a good start. They both know they need more conversations before a final answer can be reached.
3. Keep the house in the family for as long as José wants it—when they sell the house the profits (no matter what they are) will be split evenly. José will cover the pro-bate costs.	
José gets the deed to the house, his sister gets the family jewelry and a few pieces of family heirloom furniture, and his brother gets the car.	

M = Make conversations comfortable

O = One by one

N = Nurture shared goals

E = Evaluate practical solutions

Y = Yes to compassion

CONVERSATIONS WITH YOUR FINANCIAL THERAPIST

Saying yes to compassion after a family loss is so important because everyone grieves in their own way. Emotions can be all over the place, and it's easy for misunderstandings to happen. Leading with kindness helps keep the focus on supporting each other and honoring your loved one's memory, rather than getting caught up in disagreements. It makes tough conversations feel a little lighter and helps avoid lasting resentment. When you approach things with empathy and patience, it creates space for healing and finding solutions together—and that's something your loved one would likely want for all of you.

José	Sam
José tries to remember that grief looks different for everyone. He wants to be patient with emotional reactions or unexpected behaviors. As much as it is comforting for José to remain in the home, he also understands it is difficult for his siblings to keep coming back to the house where they grew up. By having compassion for them, the next family meetup will be at his brother's house.	Sam can feel herself getting frustrated with her mother's lack of knowledge on how to read a bill and bank statement. She reminds herself that this isn't a skill her mom has ever used before and takes deep breaths. Those yoga classes are coming in handy now. (See Script 20: Balance Sheets and Inner Peace.) Sam's mom leaves their first (of many) meeting feeling dumb, overwhelmed, and not ready to take on the finances. She wants to admit defeat. Instead she creates a daily affirmation, "I will be okay. I am learning and growing each day. Be Patient." They have decided to meet a few times a week over the next month to gather all the information, but once they have it, they will meet monthly to keep each other accountable and make progress on updating the finances, identifying the beneficiaries, and creating a new estate plan.

José	Sam
José remembers to take a break when needed. If tensions rise, he suggests stepping away and returning to the conversation later. A little space can help bring clarity and calm.	Sam reached out to a friend who lost her dad two years ago to reassure herself that she isn't forgetting anything. The call left her feeling like she wasn't alone.
Even during difficult conversations, José tries to choose words that show respect and understanding. A simple "I know this is hard for all of us" can go a long way.	Sam and her mom choose to take their challenging situation and see it as an opportunity to strengthen their bond.

Where Are They Now?

José is BBQing in the backyard getting ready to have his whole family over for a Sunday night dinner. It has been two years since Marta passed away and tonight they will celebrate their mother's birthday with love and laughter and a few sarcastic remarks among siblings.

After the initial meeting, the siblings, with the help of an estate planning attorney, came up with three options:

1. Have a realtor appraise the house for today's value. After seeing the sale price minus what they own on the mortgage, they can sell it and split the equity evenly.
2. What their mom says goes, at least to José. He remains in the house and fights in court to keep the house as he has been paying the mortgage, taxes, and upkeep for years. After all his Mom did say it was his.
3. José continues to live in the house, paying the mortgage, and puts in his will that when he dies or sells the house, the initial equity that

was there when his mom passed away will be divided out to his siblings. To meet the demands of the current cash his sister needs, she took the jewelry and some furniture and his brother got the deed to the car.

What Would You Do?

José and his family decide to go with option 3. While working with the estate attorney, they drafted documents to include the new agreement between them so no one could come back in a few years and say they didn't have an agreement. It costs $5,500 to draft the documents, but in the long run it will save them on potential disagreements and additional legal fees.

Where Are They Now?

Sam is driving home from visiting her mother and feeling good. They just had a wonderful visit, shared stories about their friends and family members, and talked about going on a trip together in the summer. She is feeling really proud of how far her mother has come with her confidence in making financial decisions. Here are the three options Sam came up with for her mother to gain control of her finances:

1. Sam takes over the financial role the same way Sal did and gives her mother a monthly allowance similar to the setup she had when her husband was alive.
2. Her mother and Sam meet often, learning more and more about her new financial situation, and meeting with the accountant and financial advisors once a quarter to slowly get up to speed.
3. They hire a daily money manager who pays the monthly bills, assists with tax records, balances bank records, decodes medical bills, and negotiates with creditors, basically filling in for the role of Sal.

Last Wishes and Loose Ends

The women went with option 2. Looking back on it now they have actually enjoyed the journey of learning about their finances. They still wish they had Sal around to share his wisdom, but this duo is doing okay— actually better than okay. They are thriving in life and even have remodeled the kitchen with the double oven Mom always wanted.

MONEY MANTRA

I am wealthy, focused, and empowered.
I am and have enough.
I trust my decisions and honor my growth.
Every step I take builds freedom, abundance, and peace.

XOXO, Your Future Self

DO YOU FEEL YOU/WE SHOULD SUPPORT YOUR FAMILY FINANCIALLY?

WHY OR WHY NOT?

SOURCE: LET'S TALK FINANCES CONVERSATION CARDS

CHAPTER TEN

PARENTING DOESN'T END AT 18

NAVIGATING THE NEXT CHAPTER WITH ADULT CHILDREN

CONVERSATIONS WITH YOUR FINANCIAL THERAPIST

> *This chapter features Sophia, and Madison and José.*
>
> *Sophia's daughter, Stella, now 24, has graduated college, traveled the world, and returned home to "find herself."*
>
> *Madison and José are still divorced, but need to co-parent due to increasing concerns with their son, Alex, who is now 19 years old.*
>
> *Script 21: From Crisis to Care: Working Together When It Matters Most*
>
> *Script 22: The Thermostat Standoff*

The day your child turns 18, in the law's eyes they become an adult. They can now open up credit cards, sign legal documents, and be tried as an adult if they break the law. Yet, becoming a financially responsible adult usually isn't as quick as a flick of a light switch. In the 1900s men went off to the military and returned as adult men; nowadays it is more of a gradual journey. Today, many young adults continue to rely on their parents for financial, emotional, and practical support well into their twenties and thirties. In our current environment there are many factors that contribute to this, from the cost of college tuition, rising costs of food and housing, to shifting careers and mental and/or physical illness. While for some parents it brings them closer to their kids, for others it is a financial strain not only in the short term but also to their long-term personal retirement planning. By understanding the dynamics at play, you can navigate this stage of life with care, mutual respect, and confidence.

FROM DORM ROOM TO CHILDHOOD BEDROOM: THE REMIX

Sophia

Sophia was so proud the day Stella graduated from college. She wiped tears off her face feeling like she could now relax. "My girl is ready for the world."

Parenting Doesn't End at 18

She wasn't expecting what happened next. Stella decided to take a gap year and travel the world with her graduation money. Stella planned to sell all of her belongings and embrace the world like she sees others doing on social media. As a parent, Sophia wanted to be supportive, but she also was nervous of what this would mean to Stella's future as all of her friends went off to work in their professions. Stella was always the girl who followed the rules, did the right thing, showed up for practice five minutes early and stayed late, was a straight A student, and never got into trouble. The problem was, she was burned out. Stressed out from always being on time, studying more than others, and felt she deserved a break from it all. While this wasn't according to Sophia's plan, they both agreed she could take a few months off to unwind.

A few months turned into two years. Stella, now 24, is ready to come home and re-enter the world, but with little to no money left, she decides to move in with her mom, Sophia.

Stella isn't alone in this decision to move home. More young adults today live with their parents than in the past based on a January 2024 Pew Research report. Among those ages 18–24, 57% live in a parent's home, compared with 53% in 1993.[1] While in the past it was possibly seen as a negative or failure to move back home, it has now become the norm, with over half of this age population living with their parents. In addition to living at home, data from two 2023 Pew Research Center surveys show that more than half (59%) of US parents financially support their young adult children (aged 18–34). The most common financial support provided by parents includes general household expenses (28%) and payments toward cell phone bills and streaming service subscriptions (25%). Parental financial support was less common for expenses like rent or mortgage (17%), medical expenses (15%), and education (11%).[2]

While Sophia is happy to spend time with her daughter at home, she struggles that this is a reflection on her being a bad parent when Stella was young and wonders how long her daughter will need support. Sophia's plan was to downsize to a small apartment closer to the city so she didn't have to drive as much, and save for retirement in 10 years. This was supposed to be her time to invest in her, yet she is finding herself putting her daughter first again. Sophia doesn't want money to be a source of stress, yet having Stella back in her home will cost her more money with two people using utilities, increased grocery bills, and adding Stella back to the car insurance, and so on. It could add to anywhere from $400 to $1,000/month.

BROKEN TRUST, UNBREAKABLE LOVE

Madison and José

Madison and José find themselves questioning their parenting decisions. Over the years, they've developed a co-parenting dynamic that prioritizes putting their kids first. Their approach has been to communicate openly and work collaboratively to address major challenges, creating a foundation of mutual respect and shared goals, not an easy thing to do even when married. Today is not any different, even though technically their son, Alex, is 19 years old and an adult. Both Madison and José recently have become concerned about Alex again. It was a challenge toward the end of his high school years that they chalked up to him not being a good student and ready to be out of the classroom. In fact, he barely graduated high school. The entire family clapped so loudly when he did cross the stage. Now they are trying to help guide Alex in adulthood but are being met with resistance. Both Madison and José are finding him lying on his whereabouts, he is never where he says he is going to be, and lives between their two houses or sleeps on friends' couches. José has hired him to work in the roofing business, but notices he has an issue showing up on time and has learned that he hangs out with known drug dealers in town, which leads them both to believe he is using drugs. It's time for Madison and José to talk about finding a rehab facility for Alex and how to pay for it.

Madison and José aren't alone; 48.5 million (16.7%) Americans (aged 12 and older) battled a substance use disorder in the past year. The cost of rehab varies depending on inpatient or outpatient and length of stay. The range can be from $2,000 to $30,000/month. In 2023, 40.1% of Americans 12 or older who could not get the treatment they needed in the past year said they did not seek treatment because they thought it was too expensive.[3] While Madison and José know that this money will affect their future plans financially, they are not ready for Alex to become a statistic.

Parents make sacrifices before their child is born; ask any pregnant mom who had to stop drinking, eating certain foods, take off work for doctors' appointments, and endure sleepless nights with a kicking baby. This carries into every stage of life after the baby is born, so it is no surprise that even after the law says your baby is an adult, you still have sleepless nights and financial stress over them.

Let's explore how our two families navigate these situations using the Money Mindset Method.

M = Make conversations comfortable

O = One by one

N = Nurture shared goals

E = Evaluate practical solutions

Y = Yes to compassion

Sophia and Stella	Madison and José
Stella has thrown all her bags into her old room and made herself comfortable, even dropping the air conditioning (A/C) down way past where the house using has been, without asking.	Madison and José both have had similar meetings before for major parenting conversations. They prefer to meet in person at the diner where they first met.

CONVERSATIONS WITH YOUR FINANCIAL THERAPIST

Sophia and Stella	Madison and José
Sophia is starting to feel claustrophobic in her own home, like she is the visitor. Sophia knows if she has a sit-down meeting with Stella it will lead to an argument like when she was in high school. Instead she asks Stella to take a walk with her. Conversations when they are driving or walking side by side have gone over better in the past and will get Stella outside the house!	They decided to meet on a Tuesday afternoon after work for coffee and a hard conversation.

M = Make conversations comfortable

O = One by one

N = Nurture shared goals

E = Evaluate practical solutions

Y = Yes to compassion

Sophia and Stella	Madison and José
Sophia has a lot of questions for Stella: • How long do you plan to stay here? • When are you getting a job? • How much will you be contributing to the bills? • Will you be buying groceries or do you expect me to cook and clean for you? • Is there a curfew? And what about the A/C temperature? It's way too cold in the house now and it has increased the electric bill dramatically. (See Script 22: The Thermostat Standoff.)	The first part of the conversation was sharing their concerns about what they are both noticing about Alex (See Script 21: From Crisis to Care: Working Together When It Matters Most). Madison showed up with a list of questions and concerns, which matched most of the same issues José was questioning: • Who is Alex spending time with? • Why is he not showing up for work on time? • How is he getting money if he isn't working? • Madison noticed some cash missing from her purse. • José is noticing massive mood swings. • Both have found pills missing from their homes.

Parenting Doesn't End at 18

Sophia and Stella	Madison and José
Topic: They settled on what Stella's plans are for the next six months. Sophia wrote the question on a piece of paper and put it in her pocket to touch while they walked in case she felt herself wanting to explore more of the conversation. It will help her stay focused on six-month goals.	**Topic:** How can we work together to understand what's going on with Alex and ensure he gets the help he might need?

Tip: Write your objective down and put it on a sticky note in front of you to stay focused when engaging in financial conversations.

M = Make conversations comfortable

O = One by one

N = Nurture shared goals

E = Evaluate practical solutions

Y = Yes to compassion

Sophia and Stella	Madison and José
Sophia loves Stella and wants to see her happy.	They want to present a united front to Alex to show support and care rather than judgment or blame.
Stella loves and respects her Mom, yet isn't used to having supervision again.	They research potential costs associated with treatment, including therapy, inpatient/outpatient programs, or medication.
Shared goal: To create a healthy adult relationship.	They assess whether Alex requires professional intervention, such as therapy, counseling, or rehabilitation.

CONVERSATIONS WITH YOUR FINANCIAL THERAPIST

Sophia and Stella	Madison and José
	Shared goal: To support Alex's recovery and well-being while addressing treatment options and shared financial responsibilities.

M = Make conversations comfortable

O = One by one

N = Nurture shared goals

E = Evaluate practical solutions

Y = Yes to compassion

Tip: While on a walk or a drive, play a game of "what if" to create a structured brainstorm to create options and possible opportunities to research.

Here is what Sophia and Stella, and Madison and José, came up with:

Sophia and Stella	Madison and José
What if in the next six months . . . • We establish ground rules on the A/C, times that we are coming and going so we can put the alarm on and feel safe, and agree not to leave wet laundry in the washing machine.	What if we . . . • Hire a private investigator to confirm Alex is using; that way he can't deny it. • Ask the pastor at José's church for referrals to local treatment centers.

Sophia and Stella	Madison and José
• Stella gets a part-time job bartending while three days a week she sends out résumés or attends networking meetings. • They share a car to save Stella money, but Stella pays for the gas each week. • We revisit this conversation and create another 6–12-month plan.	• Call the insurance company to find out what is covered and not covered. • Identify clear boundaries for both houses to live at home. • Discuss what the line is that they will pull back or walk away from him if he doesn't get help. • Figure out whether they can each afford to pay for treatment. They can brainstorm options on what and where to pull money from.

PROMPT

Take a minute to look at the issue in a new way.

What if we involved _____ to help solve this?

How could they contribute?

M = Make conversations comfortable

O = One by one

N = Nurture shared goals

E = Evaluate practical solutions

Y = Yes to compassion

Parenting adult children during challenging times requires compassion—not just for them, but for yourself. Start by acknowledging your feelings and understanding it's okay to feel overwhelmed. Set healthy boundaries to balance your support with your own well-being, reminding yourself that saying no is sometimes an act of love. Prioritize self-care, celebrate small wins, and replace self-criticism with gentle affirmations like "I'm doing my best." Lean on trusted friends or professionals for support, allowing others to lighten your load. Forgive yourself for not having all the answers, and embrace grace as both you and your child grow through this journey together.

Sophia and Stella	Madison and José
Sophia has decided to use the time that Stella is at her bartending job to enjoy the quiet house. She schedules her nights in on those days.	It would be really easy here to start blaming each other and/or family history. Showing compassion for each other and themselves will go a long way over the next few months.
Sophia started therapy to talk to someone about the guilty feeling she has about failing as a parent having her A student now living at home.	They can join a support group like Al-Anon or speak with a therapist who specializes in addiction-related family dynamics.
	They recognize the difference between support and enabling. Protecting your mental and financial stability is not selfish—it's necessary.

Where Are They Now?

It's been a rocky few months since Stella moved in. There have been a few blowout arguments over dirty clothes and the alarm not being put on at night, but there have also been a few sweet moments of learning about each other as people, not just parent/child.

Sophia introduced Stella to the Money Mindset Method and coached her through coming up with three options that Stella could use as guidelines to her future living situation.

Here are the three choices Stella came up with for herself:

1. Stay at home, bartend, half-ass trying to get a job, and really just buying time until she has enough money to move to Thailand.

2. Move into an old high school friend's apartment as the fourth roommate. She can't handle one more night at her mom's place.
3. Continue to live with her mom, pay half of all the bills, and slowly adjust to living back in the States with a 9–5 job.

What Would You Do?

Sophia and Stella have actually enjoyed finding each other in their adult relationship. It's been 10 months since Stella moved in; she is enjoying her new role in human resources working for an international company and helping employees move to positions all around the world. She still bartends on occasion to stay in touch with friends and build her travel fund back up while also helping Sophia with the bills around the house. They ended up going with option 3 for now and both agreed to revisit this conversation in another 6–12 months.

Where Are They Now?

Two weeks after their first meeting, Madison and José meet up again at the diner to talk about the information they have found out in the past few days. Alex was a no-show to dinner on Sunday at his grandmother's house and that was the final straw for José.

They come up with three options to present to Alex:

1. Intervention meeting with Alex and his whole family where he leaves immediately for treatment. The cost is $10,000/month for 30 days. The insurance deductible hasn't been met for the year and their kids are under José's insurance plan. José has agreed to pay for $7,000, which is his deductible, and Madison will pay the remainder of what isn't covered.

2. Do nothing. He is an adult.
3. Tell Alex he is no longer welcome to live at (either) home. He needs to find a place to live if he is not going to respect the rules. Offer to find him and pay for an outpatient support group and/or therapist if he is willing to go, but they do not force him. He is an adult.

What Would You Do?

After a lot of thinking and difficult conversations, Madison and José decided that the best thing for Alex is the intervention. Before a family dinner they gathered together and shared with Alex what was scaring them with his lifestyle and they wanted it to change today. The urgency comes from knowing how serious this situation is—it's not just about the drugs or stealing, it's about his life, his future.

Madison and José are both willing to do whatever it takes, even though the financial burden is heavy. They shared with him that they will cover the cost of rehab one time only, and this was the time. They expressed they loved him, and were ready to support him through this journey, no matter how hard it gets. He will always be their baby.

Resources: Many states offer free or low-cost treatment options. Visit your state's health department website or call the SAMHSA helpline (1-800-662-HELP).

Parenting Doesn't End at 18

MONEY MANTRA

I am wealthy, focused, and empowered.
I am and have enough.
I trust my decisions and honor my growth.
Every step I take builds freedom, abundance, and peace.

XOXO, Your Future Self

WHO
DO YOU TALK TO
ABOUT MONEY?

SOURCE: LET'S TALK FINANCES CONVERSATION CARDS

BONUS CHAPTER

HIRING AND FIRING A FINANCIAL ADVISOR

CONVERSATIONS WITH YOUR FINANCIAL THERAPIST

This chapter features Averi and William.

Averi is 10 years out of law school, age 35, consistently making "good money," paying off her student loans, vested in her firm's retirement plan, but also ready to start making her own investments. She's just not sure whom to trust or if she has enough money to even have a financial advisor.

William is post his second divorce, age 62, and has worked for years with an advisor whom he met through his parents 30 years ago. He recently met an advisor at an event who is focused on retirement planning and he wants to move his money over to the new person, yet he is nervous to upset his current advisor or disappoint his deceased parents.

Script 23: On the Run to Financial Health: Let's Talk Advisors

Script 24: Resetting Financial Goals and Advisors

We look for experts to help us in various areas of our lives; for example, we go to a doctor for health issues, the dentist to examine our teeth, or the auto mechanic to keep our car running. All of these professionals have a passion for their business, spent years in school, and in general have a vast knowledge of a specified topic. The same is true for financial professionals. The same way people have distrust, cost concerns, and feel they can "do it yourself" (DIY) is true in the financial industry. I often hear that people do not understand the different roles of financial advisors, the costs associated with what they provide, or know whom to trust. Like other professions, there are an entire spectrum of professionals, costs, and trust involved when working with a financial professional. Working with a financial professional can have a profound emotional impact, offering both relief and challenges.

TWO SIDES OF A COIN
Let's Start with the Positive Emotional Impacts

Relief and clarity: A financial professional provides structure, helping untangle overwhelming money issues and creating a clear plan for both short- and long-term planning. This can reduce anxiety and create a sense of control.

Confidence building: Gaining expert guidance helps individuals feel empowered to make informed decisions, improving their confidence in managing money.

Stress reduction: Having a trusted professional to lean on can alleviate the emotional burden of navigating complex financial situations alone.

Validation: A financial professional often normalizes financial struggles, showing clients they're not alone and providing a safe space to share concerns.

Let's Look at the Challenging Emotional Impacts

Vulnerability: Talking about money can feel uncomfortable or shameful, as it often reveals deeply personal fears or mistakes.

Resistance to change: Recommendations for lifestyle adjustments or tough decisions can trigger discomfort, guilt, or defensiveness.

Fear of judgment: Discussing finances often brings up feelings of shame, guilt, or embarrassment, especially if someone has made mistakes, accumulated debt, or lacks financial knowledge.

Lack of control: Working with a financial professional can feel like losing control, especially when emotional attachments to money conflict with recommended changes, triggering defensiveness or discomfort.

Take a look at a dollar bill; it has two different sides on it. So do our emotions with money. It is important to spend time reviewing, understanding, and appreciating both sides. The more you know about your emotions, triggers, goals, and fears about money, the more it will help navigate conversations with financial professionals.

What are the two sides of our own money? According to Nobel Prize winner in economics Daniel Kahneman, 90% of our financial decisions are emotional and only 10% are logical.[1] Let me say that again: 90% of our financial decisions are emotional and 10% logical. Does that resonate with you? It does for my clients. I recently had a client tell me she hasn't furnished her house with a kitchen table, because the one she wants is $1,500, but she just got back from a vacation that cost the same amount. Money and emotions are everywhere and it is no different than when we select a financial expert to work with.

I often get asked who are the professional people one should talk to and what are their roles. There are a lot of confusing acronyms out there. Let's get familiar with some of the more popular roles that are in the financial industry, certifications, fees, and focus areas.

Role	Certification	Typical Fees to Clients	Focus Area
Financial advisor	CFP, ChFC	1% of assets under management (AUM; total dollar amount invested or flat rates for planning) annually, or flat fees ($2,000–$5,000 per plan)	Planning, investments
Financial analyst	CFA	N/A (usually employed by firms, not directly hired by individuals)	Investments, data analysis

Hiring and Firing a Financial Advisor

Role	Certification	Typical Fees to Clients	Focus Area
Wealth manager	CPWA	0.50–1.5% of AUM, or $10,000+ annually for high-net-worth clients	High-net-worth clients
Accountant	CPA	$200–$500/hour, or $1,000–$3,000 for tax preparation	Taxes, compliance, auditing
Insurance advisor	CLU, CIC	Commission-based (varies, typically 5–10% of premium)	Risk, insurance planning
Certified Financial Therapist	CFT™	$150–$450/hour, or $2,000–$7,500 for packages	Behavioral finance
Financial coach	AFC, CFEI	$100–$300/session, or packages ($500–$2,000)	Budgeting, money management
Robo-advisor	None (platforms are automated)	0.25–0.50% of AUM annually, or $5–$15/month	Automated investment management
Credit union/ bank counselor	Certified Credit Counselor (CCC)	Often free for members, or low-cost	Budgeting, basic financial guidance
Financial planner (flat fee/hourly)	CFP, ChFC	$200–$500/hour or $1,000–$3,000 for a plan	Comprehensive financial planning
Certified divorced financial analyst	CDFA	$150–$450/hour, or $2,500–$7,500 for packages	Divorce specialist for dividing assets
Nonprofit financial counselor	AFC	Free or low cost	Debt management, budgeting
DIY tools/apps	None	Free to $15/month	Budgeting and automated investing
Estate planner	CTFA	Hourly fees of $250–$500, or $1,000–$7,000 per plan	Estate and trust planning
Loan specialist/ banker	NMLS license	No direct fees to clients; earns via interest on loans or commission from lending firms	Loan products, financing

NOTES ON CLIENT FEES

- **Financial advisor/wealth manager:** These providers often charge based on AUM. High-net-worth clients may pay higher fees for bespoke services.
- **Accountant/tax specialist:** Fees vary based on complexity, with higher costs for businesses or intricate tax situations.
- **Insurance advisor:** These providers typically do not charge direct fees but earn through commissions on policies sold.
- **Loan specialist/banker:** Clients typically don't pay upfront fees but incur costs through interest rates or lender fees embedded in loans.

* * *

Do not let this information overwhelm you; it is for reference to help you.

Now that we have established various roles and fees, let's talk about the other 90% of the role. As mentioned before, 10% of the job is performance of your money and the other 90% is emotional. How someone makes you feel is usually the larger part of the equation when working with an expert. Many of us want to find a professional who makes us feel comfortable to ask the dumb questions, feel seen and heard on our views, support our risk tolerance, and understand our opinions on various industries or alternative investments without judgments.

I recently read that men and women select advisors differently, which isn't surprising as both sexes approach a lot of things with different mindsets. Women look for in a financial advisor someone who makes them feel comfortable, empowered, and respected as an intelligent partner, similar to their romantic partners. The same study by New York Life[2] states that there are five key attributes an advisor must have to obtain and retain women clients: empathy, financial wellness, alignment, communication, and education. It's not just about financial results. However, one relevant study from the 2018 Investor Preferences Survey from the Financial Planning

Association (FPA) states that 70% of male investors rated their advisor's performance history and clear, data-driven risk management approach as "very important" in their decision-making process, with less of an importance on interpersonal skills. In fact, the top three skills were technical expertise, a proven track record, and robust risk management strategies as their top priorities when selecting a financial advisor.

Averi

Averi has it on her to-do list to speak with a financial advisor, yet she doesn't know where to start the process. After years of progressing in her career, paying down her student loans each month, and putting away money into the company's retirement plan, she has also noticed that she has a nice nest egg building in her savings account. In the past she tried to meet with a financial professional, but they told her she didn't have enough money to work with them, leaving a bitter taste in her mouth. Since then, she has felt embarrassed to ask again for help. She isn't alone; asking for support and being turned down doesn't feel good. Today, she is struggling with how to find a financial professional who fits her needs without making her feel ashamed of her lack of financial knowledge.

Today, females control 51% of the personal wealth in the United States, about $14 trillion. That amount is expected to reach $22 trillion within 10 years and then increase even more rapidly as women receive funds from the "great wealth transfer."[3] Over the next 20 years, trillions of dollars transferred from baby boomers to younger generations will create opportunities for younger Americans to reshape their finances. Understanding how to work with younger generations and different client types will be essential for advisors to obtain and retain clients.

Averi will work through the Money Mindset Method to explore what needs she has for an advisor, how to obtain one who understands her, and who can provide her with a high rate of return for her money.

William

William has also decided to use the Money Mindset Method to work through how or if he should change advisors. Will is headed into a new chapter of his life. Recently divorced for the second time, he moved into an over-55 community, is meeting new friends, and enjoying a fresh start in life. While he is feeling young at heart, he knows retirement is coming soon and wonders if he will be financially ready for it. A few years ago, his parents passed away, leaving him a nice inheritance that will allow him to retire into a nicer lifestyle than if he had to depend only on his savings. He has been with his current advisor for 30 years. In fact, it is the same advisor his parents used. Over the years, his advisor has treated him nicely, provided steady returns for both his parents and himself, yet he still feels like he is the child in the relationship, not the primary client. Recently, at an event at his new clubhouse there was a presentation from Jorge, a financial advisor who specializes in retirement planning. William's interest is piqued, but he is unsure how to fire his current advisor and what the steps are to hire a new one and at the same time wondering what his parents would think of this move. He isn't alone in having the urge to find his own advisor after the passing of his parents; more than 70% of heirs involved in the great wealth transfer have stated they are likely to fire or change financial advisors after inheriting their parents' wealth.[4]

M = Make conversations comfortable

O = One by one

N = Nurture shared goals

E = Evaluate practical solutions

Y = Yes to compassion

Make the conversation comfortable, but with whom? Sometimes the hardest part of having a challenging conversation is knowing who to talk to. Additionally, it may take a few tries to find the right person for the specific topic at hand. When you engage with another person for a personal conversation, make sure they have a personal interest in you, are willing to make the time to talk to you, and keep you accountable if required. Averi is ready to talk about finding an advisor, investing her money, and taking the next steps, but she is unsure on where to begin. After brainstorming for a few days, she settles on talking to her coworker Isabella at work, whom she also sees as a friend, to see how she is approaching investing her money.

William is going to have two conversations. One will be with Jorge, the retirement specialist he met the other day to learn more about his practice. The other conversation will be with his current advisor to notify them he is leaving or that he is interested in restructuring the way they are currently conducting business to empower him to feel more comfortable being their client.

Averi	William with Potential New Planner	William with Current Advisors
Averi and Isabella are peers. They often find themselves chatting in the halls, grabbing lunch when time allows, or going for a run on the weekends together. On their run this weekend, Averi brought up the topic of working with a financial advisor. It was in a casual way to test out the waters to see if this was a topic they could talk about and if Isabella had knowledge about. Running side by side it wasn't such an intense question.	Jorge called William after the meeting and set up a lunch at the same club where they met a few weeks earlier. This was familiar territory for William. He knew the menu, the staff, the layout of the room, what to wear, and so on. Jorge has worked in finance for years and knows that creating a safe place for a conversation for the client is important to building trust and comfort for a new relationship. Jorge is also aware that meeting in a known spot for William means that the purpose of the meeting is not for digging into the exact numbers, but to learn more about William's background, religion/culture, and experiences.	William sends an email to his current advisors, now a father/son team, that he would like to meet to explore the idea of retiring in the next five years. He receives a calendar invite to a Zoom link for a month from now.

CONVERSATIONS WITH YOUR FINANCIAL THERAPIST

M = Make conversations comfortable

O = One by one

N = Nurture shared goals

E = Evaluate practical solutions

Y = Yes to compassion

When you are exploring a new topic, a lot of questions or uncertainty might come to mind. Do a brainstorming session to write down all of your thoughts, concerns, and questions and then see if there is a common theme to focus on.

Averi	William
Questions Averi has for Isabella: • How did you find your financial advisor? • Do I need an advisor or a planner? • Do I have enough money to hire one? • How much does working with a financial professional cost? Is it worth it? • What if I don't know anything about the stock market should I even be investing in it? • How often do you meet with an advisor? (See Script 23: On the Run to Financial Health: Let's Talk Advisors.)	Questions William has for his new and old financial advisors: • When can I retire? • What will retirement look like for me? • Can I afford to retire in five years? • What will taxes be when I retire? • What am I doing now to set myself up for retirement? • Can I give my kids money? • Who's my new beneficiary now that I am single again? • What is the difference between the financial advisor I am using now versus a retirement plan specialist? (See Script 24: Resetting Financial Goals and Advisors.)
Topic: How do I know if hiring a financial advisor is the right step for me?	**Topic:** What financial strategies will help me achieve the retirement I want?

M = Make conversations comfortable

O = One by one

N = Nurture shared goals

E = Evaluate practical solutions

Y = Yes to compassion

Shared goals create a win-win situation, bringing everyone together to work toward the same positive outcome. It's all about teamwork and finding solutions that benefit everyone involved.

Averi	William
Averi's goal is to grow her wealth, feel confident in financial decisions, and ensure she's making smart investments.	William wants his advisor(s) to create a focused, long-term plan that aligns with his retirement timeline and goals.
The right financial advisor for Averi is one who provides valuable advice, helps clients succeed, and builds long-term relationships.	William wants to maximize retirement savings by having his advisor(s) identify tax-efficient strategies, investment options, and withdrawal plans to ensure financial security in his retirement.
	Both advisors share the goal of ensuring William's financial future is secure but approach it from different angles—one focusing on the long-term retirement horizon, while the other manages overall wealth and legacy.

M = Make conversations comfortable

O = One by one

N = Nurture shared goals

E = Evaluate practical solutions

Y = Yes to compassion

CONVERSATIONS WITH YOUR FINANCIAL THERAPIST

Averi	William
Averi made an appointment with the financial advisor Isabella recommended to her.	William considers keeping his money where it is today: have a review with the current team and change nothing.
They reviewed the list of questions Averi came into the meeting with.	William also considers having a review with the current team about what his retirement planning is, ask to make a few updates, including working and following up with the son versus the father, as he feels a stronger connection with the son.
The advisor asked Averi goal and risk questions.	William considers moving his retirement accounts over to Alex and keeping the other accounts with the current advisors.
Together, they outlined the next steps if they worked together on the cost, risk, and possible returns. Averi's next step is to interview two more advisors before making a decision on whom to go with.	William considers moving all his accounts to Alex and his team, giving him a fresh start on finances.

M = Make conversations comfortable

O = One by one

N = Nurture shared goals

E = Evaluate practical solutions

Y = Yes to compassion

Averi	William
Yes, it is okay that Averi is not a financial whiz. This is not her field of expertise.	William needs to recognize that his financial needs have evolved and that it's okay to prioritize his future over past loyalties to his parents.

Averi	William
Averi needs to let go of any shame and past mistakes (we all make them).	William needs to remind himself that this decision is about securing the best future for himself and his family.
Yes, Averi needs to ask more questions and learn about investing in a curious way.	William needs to honor the value his parents' advisors brought over the years.

Where Are They Now?

It's six months later and Averi has finished a run with Isabella. They were swapping notes on new stocks they are following, which social media accounts they love to learn from, and how proud they are of growing their skills in finance. Averi considered three options:

1. Sign the paperwork to work with the first advisor she met.
2. Decide to DIY it with the help of experts on social media.
3. Interview three financial professionals, including advisors and planners.

What Would You Do?

Averi went with option 3 and met with a few different people to see whom she felt the most comfortable with, the costs of working together that felt like it had value, and learned more about the various ways to invest in stocks, bonds, alternative investments, and so on. She ended up hiring the second person she met with. They meet once a quarter to grow their relationship and Averi's understanding of investing. In addition, she started following a few experts on social media to keep up with daily information and learned about Savvy Ladies (www.savvyladies.org) a non-profit empowering women with financial knowledge. Together with all of this data she is able to now make a more educated decision on where to invest her money.

Where Are They Now?

William is sitting at the coffee table talking to his oldest son about his new investment strategies and how excited he is to not only be ready to retire in a few more years but also about the amount of golf and travel he is going to get to do. He shared his three options:

1. Do nothing: the conversations would be too difficult and too much work to move money around or hurt anyone's feelings especially people his parents respected.
2. Move over his retirement accounts to Jorge and keep the investment accounts with the current advisors.
3. Move all his accounts over to Jorge.

What Would You Do?

William went with option 2. He still had an emotional attachment to his current advisors and they were performing for him, but he also wanted to branch out on his own and explore working with Alex for retirement planning. He left the last meeting with Alex feeling proud that he made the right decision for himself. This split of assets enables him to work with both advisors and over time to see if anything additional needs to shift or change for future money management while building confidence in his current relationship with money.

Hiring and Firing a Financial Advisor

MONEY MANTRA

I am wealthy, focused, and empowered.
I am and have enough.
I trust my decisions and honor my growth.
Every step I take builds freedom, abundance, and peace.

XOXO, Your Future Self

CONCLUSION

OWN IT

YOUR RELATIONSHIP WITH MONEY ONE CONVERSATION AT A TIME

Here we are at the end of the book. The time has come for us to part ways. I hope that you have enjoyed the journey as much as I have enjoyed writing the book. My wish for you is that you are leaving here feeling more confident in your future relationship with money. Building this new relationship will take time, patience, and understanding, both for yourself and others around you. If you find this book helpful, it is a good idea to share it with your loved ones whom you will be having these financial conversations with. It also can be used as a way to open up the topic of talking about money.

The goal of this book is to help guide you to talk about money, have a little more understanding about the emotions that come with the topic, provide a framework to support the conversations, and give examples of how it can be done successfully.

Before you go, let's break it down one more time and what the results are if you use the **Money Mindset Method to grow your financial mindset.**

Conclusion

M = Make Conversations Comfortable

- Talking about money takes practice.
- Practice leads to progress.
- Progress leads to gaining new abilities and skills.

O = One by One

- Focus on one topic at a time.
- This is not the time to fix all the problems in the world.
- With each issue you focus on, solve for, it will free you up to tackle the next one.

N = Nurture Shared Goals

- Collaboration builds mutual respect and a stronger relationship.
- Regular communication fosters understanding and minimizes misunderstandings.
- Achievements feel more rewarding when both parties contribute.

E = Evaluate Practical Solutions

- Sometimes you will want to think outside the box for a solution.
- Asking or seeking support is cool.
- Discovering a possible way to solve a problem feels good.

Y = Yes to Compassion

- You will not always get it right the first time. Try, try again.
- Keep having the possible awkward, tough, uncomfortable conversations. Don't get discouraged.
- Be kind to yourself and others.

CONVERSATIONS WITH YOUR FINANCIAL THERAPIST

As you move forward, remember that the journey doesn't end here and *whatever you are doing right now you are getting better at it*. Financial well-being is a continuous process of growth, learning, and adapting. Celebrate the milestones, forgive the missteps, and keep the conversation alive. The roller coaster of life may throw unexpected twists your way, but now you're equipped to ride with confidence, compassion, and clarity.

The future is yours to own. Let's make it one filled with freedom, fulfillment, and financial peace of mind.

—XOXO, *Erika*

SCRIPTS

SCRIPT 1: MAKE THE DAMN CALL!

Scene: Madison (M) sitting in the living room on the couch with her laptop on her lap looking at her credit card bill. She eyes her phone sitting next to her for over an hour then, gathers a bit of courage, and dials the customer service number listed on the back of her credit card and reaches the credit card operator (CCO).

CCO: (cheerfully) Thank you for calling ABC BANKING. My name is Jamie. How can I assist you today?

M: (nervously) Hi, Jamie, this is Madison. I've been a cardholder with you for over a year now. I'm calling to see if I could get a reduction on my credit card APR.

CCO: Thank you for your loyalty, Madison. Let me check your account details. Please hold for a moment. (pause) Yes, I see you've been a customer, paying the minimum amount monthly on time. Can you tell me why you're seeking a rate reduction today?

SCRIPTS

M: I've been researching and noticed that there are several credit card companies offering lower rates. For example, XYZ Bank is offering 18% APR, which is significantly lower than my current rate with you. I was wondering if you could match or offer a better rate. ·

CCO: I appreciate you sharing that information. Let me see what I can do. (pause) I can offer you a reduced APR of 20%. How does that sound?

M: (excited it was working, but determined) I appreciate the offer, but 20% is still higher than I was hoping for. I've been a loyal customer and always paid on time. Could you reconsider and possibly lower it further, maybe closer to 18%?

CCO: I understand your concern, Madison. Unfortunately, that's the best rate I can offer at the moment.

M: (politely adds) Could you explain why the rate can't be lowered further? Or pass me to a manager I could speak with about this?

CCO: I understand your frustration. I can connect you to a supervisor, but before I do that, would you be interested in any other benefits, like bonus points or additional incentives, if we can't adjust the rate?

M: That could be an option, but my main goal is to reduce the interest rate. I'd still like to speak with a supervisor, please.

CCO: Certainly, Madison. Please hold while I transfer you. (pause)

M: (give out a big exhale—it's working)

* * *

Supervisor: (politely) Hi, Madison, this is John, the supervisor. I understand you're looking to reduce your APR. Let me take a closer look at your account. (pause) I see you've been an exemplary customer. While the 20% APR is the standard reduction, I can offer you a temporary rate reduction to 18% for the next six months. Does that work for you?

SCRIPTS

M: That's helpful, John. Thank you. I'll take the temporary reduction for now.

Supervisor: Glad to hear that works for you, Madison. We appreciate your business. Is there anything else I can assist you with today?

M: No, that's all for now. Thank you for your help! I'll chat with you again in six months.

End Scene

SCRIPT 2: DON'T LET YOUR MIND BE THE WEAKNESS MUSCLE

Scene: Gabe (G) stands in front of a mirror, slightly anxious but determined.

G: All right, Gabe. Here we go. First off (pauses) I appreciate everything mom and dad have done for me. I wouldn't even be standing here without them.

(nods to himself)

G: But now? It's on me. I need to take ownership of my future. Time to step up.

(laughs, shakes his head)

G: I'm probably gonna mess this up. I mean, let's be real—bills, rent, groceries . . . it's all new. But that's okay. It's normal. People do it every day. I can do it, too.

(points at his reflection, a bit more confident)

G: You can do this. One step at a time, take the time to learn from the mistakes, ask Mom and Dad questions when needed, and just do it.

End Scene

SCRIPT 3: IS IT TIME TO SHIFT MY CAREER? ADVICE NEEDED

Scene: Averi (A) is sitting in her office, looking at the clock as the time winds down on a gray gloomy day. Averi is trying to decide on what is the best career move, so she picks up her phone to call Henry (H), an old law school friend who recently made a big career shift by starting his own firm to ponder what it would be like to work for herself.

A: (on speaker phone) Hey, Henry, it's Averi. How are you?

H: (cheerful) Averi! Long time, no talk. I'm good, just the usual chaos over here. How about you?

A: (laughs) You know, the same chaos but a different day. I just wrapped up a big case, and things are finally slowing down a bit. I wanted to see if you have time to catch up.

H: Of course! What's going on?

A: Well, I've been thinking a lot about my career lately. You know me—I don't love change, but I've been feeling stuck. I've been at the same firm for 10 years, and while it's been good in many ways, I'm starting to wonder if it's time to move on.

H: (intrigued) Hmm, that's a big thought. What's making you feel that way?

A: Honestly, it's a mix of things. I'm happy here for the most part—I like my colleagues, feel valued, and I'm making really good money. But that's also part of what scares me.

H: (curious) Scares you how?

A: If I leave to start something new, like my own practice, what if it doesn't work out? What if I can't make enough to cover my expenses?

SCRIPTS

The idea of walking away from a stable paycheck and possibly ending up broke is terrifying.

H: (supportive) I hear you. That fear is real, but it's also part of the process when you're considering a big change. Have you looked at what your financial cushion would look like if you took the leap?

A: A little. I've saved up a good amount, but I keep wondering if it's enough. And what if I misjudge the costs of going out on my own?

H: (reassuring) Those are valid questions, but they're also things you can plan for. The key is to do your homework and create a solid plan before making any decisions. Let's meet up, and I'll walk you through what worked for me.

A: (relieved) That would be amazing. I just need someone who's been through it to give me the real picture—the good, the bad, and the ugly.

H: (chuckles) You know I don't sugarcoat. How about our old spot from law school?

A: Perfect. I've got a light week coming up, so I can actually leave work at a decent hour. Does 5 p.m. on Thursday work for you?

H: Thursday at 5 p.m. it is. Don't stress, Averi—we'll figure this out.

A: Thanks, Henry. I really appreciate it.

H: Anytime. See you Thursday!

End Scene

SCRIPT 4: LEVELING UP: A CONVERSATION ON PROMOTIONS IN THE WORKPLACE

Setting: Gabe (G) has scheduled a meeting with his human resources partner, Louisa (L), to discuss his career development and the details of his recent promotion. They're meeting in her office on a Tuesday morning, a time Gabe knows she's available and focused.

L: Hi, Gabe, thanks for coming in. How's everything going?

G: Thanks for meeting with me, Louisa. Things are good. I wanted to follow up on my promotion and talk through some questions I have about my growth here at the company.

L: Of course, I'm happy to help. Congratulations again on the promotion—you've been doing great work. What's on your mind?

G: I appreciate that. I'm excited about the new responsibilities, especially the management experience with the interns. But I'm also trying to make sure this aligns with my long-term goals.

L: That's great to hear. What are you thinking in terms of your goals?

G: Well, ultimately, I'd like to grow into a leadership role here—maybe even an executive position down the line. At the same time, I want to feel respected for my contributions and maintain a good work–life balance. I've seen some colleagues burn out, and I want to make sure I avoid that.

L: That's a thoughtful approach, Gabe. Leadership growth is definitely a priority for us as well, and we're excited to see you develop those skills. Did you have specific concerns about the promotion?

SCRIPTS

G: A couple of things. The scope of work is increasing significantly, which I'm fine with, but I'm unclear on when the salary increase will take effect. It's hard to plan ahead without knowing.

L: I understand how that can feel uncertain. With the company merger, there's been some restructuring, and we're aligning compensation plans with the new budget cycle. Your raise is approved, but the timeline is tied to next quarter's updates. So give me a few more months to sort it out, but it is coming.

G: Got it. Thanks for clarifying. In the meantime, I want to make sure I'm positioned to succeed in this role and continue growing. Are there resources or mentorship opportunities I could tap into?

L: Absolutely. We have leadership development programs that I think would be a great fit for you. I can also connect you with a senior manager who could serve as a mentor to help you navigate this transition.

G: That sounds great. One more thing—I want to make sure I'm managing the increased workload effectively. Are there strategies or tools you'd recommend for maintaining balance while stepping into a more demanding role?

L: That's a smart question. Time management will be key. I'd suggest blocking time on your calendar for focused work and building in breaks to recharge. I'll also check in with your manager to ensure the workload remains reasonable.

G: Thanks, Louisa. I appreciate your support. This helps me feel more confident about what's ahead.

L: I'm glad to hear that. Let's schedule a follow-up in a month to see how things are going. Sound good?

G: Perfect. Thanks again, Louisa.

End Scene

SCRIPTS

SCRIPT 5: THE CODEWORD IS _____

Scene: Madison (M) and José (J) are learning how to proactively communicate with each other about the topic of money. Before they start, Madison wants to create a code word for when things get emotional. They are sitting at their small kitchen table after finishing their dinner. Madison is showing a small baby bump. José looks slightly nervous as they prepare to talk about finances.

M: (rubbing her belly, glancing at the budget spreadsheet in front of them) Okay, babe. So, I think before we even dive into this, we need . . . a plan. Like, if it starts getting too intense.

J: (nods quickly) Yeah, for sure. I mean, I don't want to stress you out . . . or me. But we have to talk about this stuff. It's important.

M: Exactly. So how about we come up with a code word? Something silly we can use if things get heated, or if we just need a break. My friend told me she does this with her boyfriend and it works well.

J: (laughs out loud) A code word? Like, pineapple or something?

M: (smirking) Hmm, close! But what about . . . pickles? It's random enough. And I've been craving them like crazy.

J: (laughs) Pickles, huh? All right, pickles it is. So if either of us says "pickles," we hit pause, right?

M: (nods) Yep, we stop. But it's not to avoid the conversation forever. (pauses) We'll take a break—like a walk around the block or put on some music—and then come back with a fresh mindset and maybe even a new idea to solve the problem.

SCRIPTS

J: (rubbing his chin, thinking) I like that. So, we say "pickles," take a break for, what . . . 10 minutes?

M: (grinning) Yeah, 10 minutes sounds good. We'll set a timer, and after that, we'll come back to it. Maybe even dance it out if we need to shake off the tension. What do you think?

J: (smiling) I'm down for a little dance party if it comes to that. I like this plan, Madi, especially if it's gonna help keep things from blowing up. I don't like fighting with you.

M: (laughing) Exactly! So . . . let's get started. And remember—"pickles" if we need it.

J: (playfully raises an eyebrow) Pickles. Got it.

End Scene

SCRIPTS

SCRIPT 6: BLENDING FAMILY, FINANCES, AND FOOD BILLS

Scene: Using the yours/mine/ours planning, William (W), who's a conscientious father of two sons from a previous marriage, and Sophia (S), who is practical and budget conscious, have a conversation about how to handle the extra expenses of food with step-kids while cooking dinner.

W: (calmly) Hey, Sophia. I wanted to talk to you about the grocery budget.

S: (without looking up) What about it?

W: Well, I've noticed we're spending more lately in that joint category, throwing off "our" account a little each month.

S: (stops chopping, turns to face William) You mean you noticed we spend more on groceries when your kids are here? (pretends to put a shocked face on)

W: Hmmm . . . I know they are growing boys and food expenses have increased almost as much as their appetites. They are here every other week.

S: (sighs) William, I get that they eat more these days, but it's not fair to expect me to cover those extra costs from *my* money. We already have a tight "our" budget.

W: I'm not saying it should all come from you. We can figure it out together. Maybe cut back on some other expenses to cover the food costs more?

S: (crosses arms) It's not just about cutting back. It feels like I'm the one always compromising. I work hard for my money, and I don't think it's fair to spend extra on something that's not my responsibility.

SCRIPTS

W: (softens) I understand where you're coming from, honey. But they're my sons, and providing for them is important to me. I want them to feel comfortable and fed here. Can't we find a middle ground?

S: (pauses, then sighs) Look, I'm not trying to be difficult. I know they're important to you. I love them, too. Maybe we can set a fixed amount that we both contribute for the weeks they are not here, and anything additional on the weeks they are here, comes from your "mine bank" account.

W: (nods) That sounds fair. Let's sit down and go through the budget together. We'll figure out a way that works for both of us.

S: (smiles slightly) Okay, let's do that.

W: (reaches out to hold Sophia's hand) We are in this together, forever.

End Scene

SCRIPTS

SCRIPT 7: THE STROLLER SHOWDOWN: FUNCTION VERSUS FASHION

Scene: Sophia (S) and William (W) have a conversation on purchasing a stroller for the baby. The couple is sitting on the couch scrolling through their phones when Sophia stops to show William a picture of the latest trendy stroller on social media.

S: (showing her phone to William) Look at this, honey! Isn't this stroller amazing? It has the one-push close, the flexible handle, *everything*! Plus, it looks so chic. I can already picture myself pushing it down the street. (she smiles)

W: (glancing at the phone) It does look nice, sweetie. But it costs $800. That's a lot for a stroller that the baby is going to outgrow, don't you think?

S: (tilts her head) I know it's a bit pricey, but it's a social media gold. I'd be "one of those Moms" I see online. It's about making a statement. I've dreamed of this moment for so long, and I want it to be perfect.

W: (pauses, thinking) I get that. But remember my coworker Steve? He's giving away his old stroller. It's in great condition and perfectly functional. Babies don't care about brand names, and soon enough, it's going to have food and stains all over it anyway. Let's save the money for diapers.

S: (sighs) I know you're right about the practical side, but it's not just about that for me. I've always imagined having this beautiful, stylish stroller with my hair breezing in the wind as I stroll my perfect baby down the street looking and feeling fantastic. Right now, buying it would feel like a reward for all the hard work we've put in to get here. That I can be "that mom."

SCRIPTS

W: (smiling gently) I hear you. I do. But do we really want to spend $800 on a stroller when we could save that money for something else our baby might need? There are so many other expenses coming our way. Just look at my boys—they don't remember what stroller they were in and we both know the money could be used on better things.

S: (nodding slowly) I get what you're saying. It's just hard to let go of that dream. Maybe we can find a middle ground? What if we look for a stylish but more affordable stroller, let's say $300? That way, we don't break the bank but still get something we both like. You can keep Steve's stroller in your car as a backup.

W: (relieved) That sounds like a good compromise. Let's do some more research and see if we can find something that meets both our needs. I want you to feel proud and happy, but I also want us to be smart with our money.

S: (smiling) Deal. We'll find something that works for both of us. Thanks for understanding, William.

W: Always. We're in this together, and we'll make it work. (leans over and gives her a kiss).

End Scene

SCRIPTS

SCRIPT 8: NEW ADDITION, NEW EQUATIONS?

Scene: For Sophia (S) and William (W), having a baby on the way feels it is time to review their financial situation and make some possible adjustments to include the new joint family member. Will has recently received a large promotion and now makes close to double what Sophia does. They are sitting together in the living room for their Sunday financial meeting. There's a comfortable but slightly nervous energy in the air as Sophia takes a deep breath, preparing to initiate an important conversation.

S: Hey, babe, I've been thinking . . . with the baby on the way, I think it's time we talk about how we handle our finances overall. I know we've been doing the 50/50 split, but things are about to change big time and I am feeling really feeling really nervous.

W: (looking up from the budget sheet, a bit curious but open) Yeah, I figured this conversation was coming. I mean, diapers, baby clothes . . . it's all gonna add up. What're you thinking?

S: Well, I've been looking at everything, and with maternity leave coming up and the extra expenses, I'm not sure a 50/50 split makes sense anymore. Maybe we could move to more of a this-or-that setup instead of splitting everything down the middle?

W: (furrows his brow slightly) Okay, I hear you. But . . . how exactly would that work? And, you know, I don't want anything to change for the boys. They've got school, sports, all their usual stuff. How will this affect what I'm already covering for them?

S: (nods, understanding his concern) I totally get that, and I don't want to take anything away from your boys. They're a huge part of our lives, and I know how important it is for you to keep things stable for them.

I'm thinking we could start by dividing responsibilities. Like, instead of splitting every bill, maybe I take over utilities and baby-related expenses while you cover the mortgage and groceries?

W: (pauses, thinking it over) Okay, so let's make a list of things and put names next to it. But what about things like medical bills for the baby or saving for a college fund? Are we sharing that?

S: (nods) Yeah, we'd share those. We can sit down and figure out how much we need to set aside each month, then agree on what makes sense for both of us to contribute. That way, it doesn't fall all on one person. We'll need to be flexible as things change, but the goal is to make sure neither of us feels overwhelmed by the new expenses.

W: (leans back, ponders) Hmm. I like that. It feels more like teamwork than just splitting things down the middle. And I appreciate you thinking about how it'll work with the boys. As long as we're both still able to contribute fairly without stretching too thin, I'm on board. But we'll need to keep this conversation going as things can shift once the baby's here, especially with surprise costs.

S: (smiling softly) Exactly, we'll keep checking in. It's not set in stone, but I feel like it'll give us both more clarity. That way, we're each responsible for certain things, and we can keep supporting the whole family, including the new baby.

W: Alright, let's give it a shot. I'm in.

S: Deal. We'll try it, and if something feels off, we'll adjust. The most important thing is we're in this together and keep talking about it.

W: (smiles, reaching for her hand) We've got this.

End Scene

SCRIPTS

SCRIPT 9: RUFF DECISIONS: EXPLORING DOG OWNERSHIP

Scene: One evening while waiting for a very slow elevator to arrive Gabe (G) strikes up a conversation with his neighbor Tom (T), who has a playful puppy seeking attention, about what it is really like to own a dog.

G: (walks toward the elevator banks) Hey, Tom, how's it going? (pets the dog) Max, you look happy as ever.

T: (smiling) Hey, Gabe! Yeah, Max is always full of energy. We're just heading out for our evening walk. What's up?

G: Actually, I was hoping to catch you. I've been thinking about getting a dog myself and wanted to ask you a few questions. Do you have a minute?

T: Of course! Fire away.

G: Great, thanks. First off, what's it really like having a dog? I mean, really like, the day-to-day stuff.

T: (pauses) Well, it's definitely a commitment. You need to be prepared for daily walks, feeding, grooming, and lots of playtime. Dogs need a lot of attention and care, but they also give a lot of love in return. It can be a challenge on some days when work is also taking up a lot of your time, but I still wouldn't trade him for the world.

G: (nods his head) I can see that. What about the costs? How much do you spend on things like a dog walker?

T: Honestly, it adds up pretty quick. For a dog walker, I pay about $20 per walk. There are also costs for food, vet visits, grooming, and toys. His food is $90 for a 30-pound bag that lasts him 1–1.5 months, insurance is $48/ month for peace of mind to help with big vet bills, poop bags/toys/treats

SCRIPTS

probably run about $30–$50/month, and another $160/month for dog walker or doggie day care. It's important to have a financial cushion for unexpected expenses, too. We had a few of those when he was a puppy. I would probably say all in I spend $350/month or about $4,000/year.

G: (nods) Hmmm . . . definitely sounds like it can add up pretty quick. Are there good dog parks or places nearby where I can take the dog to run around? I feel bad if the dog was inside all day alone.

T: Definitely! There's a great dog park about 10 minutes from here. Max loves it there. It's a good way for dogs to socialize and burn off some energy. Plus, there are a few smaller parks within a short walk that are dog-friendly.

G: That sounds perfect. Would you say it's worth it? Would you do it all over again if you had the choice?

T: Absolutely. Having Max has been one of the best decisions I've made. He brings so much joy and companionship. But it's important to be ready for the responsibility. It's not just about the fun moments; it's about being there for them, rain or shine. Even on nights when you want to stay out all night you still need to come home to this guy. I'm thankful my girlfriend can work from home some days and helps out often.

G: Thanks, Tom. That's really helpful. I've been on the fence, but hearing your experience gives me a better idea of what to expect.

T: Anytime, Gabe. If you have more questions or need advice, just let me know. And if you decide to get a dog, Max and I will be here to welcome you to the club!

End Scene

SCRIPT 10: BREAKING UP AND BREAKING EVEN: THE HOUSE THAT WAS OURS

Setting: Averi (A) and Sam (S) are sitting in their usual booth at the local diner. The atmosphere is heavy with unspoken tension, but both are committed to having an honest conversation. Just as long as eye contact is not needed.

S: (nervously stirring her coffee) Thanks for meeting me, Averi. I know this isn't easy for either of us.

A: (calm but firm) You're right—it's not. But it's important we figure this out, especially about the house. I love that place. It's home to me.

S: (sighs) I know I messed up, and I take full responsibility for what happened. I don't want to make things harder for you, but I also don't know where to start with this. I need to move back into the house I bought with my money.

A: (nodding) Well, for starters, I'm not leaving the house. It's been my home too for the past eight years. I've paid half the mortgage, handled repairs, and put in money for renovations. Just because it's in your name doesn't mean it's all yours.

S: (hesitant) I hear you. I know you've contributed a lot, and it wouldn't be fair to ignore that. But legally, I'm not sure what rights you have to the house.

A: (frustrated) That's one of the things we need to figure out. What I do know is that I've invested time, money, and effort into making it a home. I'm not walking away empty-handed because of *your* mistake.

S: (sincerely) I don't want that either and I feel this conversation is about to take a turn that neither of us came here for, so let's refocus and start with what we know and what we still need answers to.

A: (pulls out her phone and opens the notes app) Good idea. Let's start with the facts.

Facts They Know

- The house is legally owned by Sam.
- Averi has lived there and paid half the mortgage and expenses for eight years.
- Averi also contributed $20,000 for renovations early on.
- Sam is already living with her new partner at her home.
- The house is close to Averi's office, and she works late hours, making it convenient for her.

Questions They Need to Answer

- What are Averi's legal rights to the house after eight years of cohabitation?
- Can Averi claim any equity in the house based on her financial contributions?
- Is it possible for Averi to buy the house outright from Sam?
- If Averi stays, how will they handle the mortgage and ownership transfer?
- What happens if they can't agree—would they need mediation or legal intervention?

S: (nodding) Hmmm . . . okay, those are solid points. I'll reach out to a real estate lawyer to see what the options are unless you know someone already.

SCRIPTS

A: (softly) Thanks. I just need to know I have a voice in this. It's not about revenge, Sam. I just want to protect what I've built here. I can ask around at the office.

S: (gently) I get it. I hurt you, and I'm not trying to push you out, but at the same time I am not going to walk away from the home either. It wouldn't make sense financially for me to do that no matter how much I screwed up.

A: (with a small smile) True. Fine . . .

S: (sincerely) We'll make it right, Averi. I owe you that.

End Scene

SCRIPTS

SCRIPT 11: NAVIGATING AND COLLABORATING A DIVORCE

Setting: Madison (M) and José (J) are sitting on the couch at the dining room table after putting their kids to bed. It's a calm evening, and they've decided to have an open conversation about their divorce and how to make it as smooth as possible for their children.

M: (takes a deep breath) José, I know this isn't easy for either of us, but I want to say I appreciate that we're both putting the kids first in this.

J: (nods) Yeah, I feel the same. Whatever happens, they deserve stability and love from both of us. I don't want them to feel like they're stuck in the middle.

M: Me neither. That's why I've been looking into collaborative divorce. It's supposed to be less adversarial—more about working together to figure out what's fair.

J: (curious) Collaborative divorce? What's that?

M: It's where we each have our own lawyers, but the goal is to negotiate everything in a way that avoids going to court. We'd also bring in neutral experts if needed, like a financial planner or child specialist, to help us figure out the best arrangements for the kids and our finances. It's what our neighbors down the street did and they are on good terms still a year later.

J: (thoughtful) That sounds better than fighting it out. I don't want to spend a fortune on lawyers when we could use that money for the kids.

M: Exactly. I was thinking we could start by listing all of our expenses and assets to figure out what we need for two households.

J: (nodding) That makes sense. We'll need to budget for two sets of bills— rent, utilities, groceries—and still make sure the kids have what they need. (nervously) That sounds like a lot!

234

SCRIPTS

M: Yeah. And we should also talk about things like who's going to cover their school fees, extracurriculars, and medical expenses. Maybe we could just set up a joint account for those shared costs?

J: (smiling slightly) A joint account for the kids? I like that idea. It keeps things simple.

M: And we'd each contribute to it based on what we can afford/agree on each year. Speaking of that, I know this might feel awkward, but I think we should be honest about our incomes and expenses. That way, we can come up with something fair.

J: (sighs) Yeah, it's not my favorite topic, but you're right. We need to know where we stand financially to make this work.

M: (gently) It's about giving the kids the best we can in both homes. They shouldn't feel like they're losing out just because we're splitting up.

J: True. And about custody—what do you think?

M: (smiles) I don't want to give up any time, but I know it's important they have time with both of us. Maybe we start with a 50/50 schedule and adjust if we need to?

J: (nodding) That's what I was thinking, too. We just need to stay flexible and keep talking as their needs change.

M: (smiling) I think we can do this, José. It won't be easy, but as long as we're honest and keep the kids at the center, we'll figure it out.

J: (smiles back) Agreed. Can you call the—what did you call them? Collaborative attorney people and set up a meeting?

M: Sounds like a plan. Thanks for being open to this, José.

J: Thanks for bringing it up, Madison. We will get through this together—for them.

End Scene

SCRIPT 12: THE GREAT BACK-TO-SCHOOL BUDGET DEBATE

Setting: Madison (M) and José (J) are sitting at a picnic table, while Alex runs around the basketball court during practice, but the real event isn't on the field—it's the annual back-to-school conversation that is about to go down between the two of them. Overall, they have been getting along regarding the kids, but back-to-school spending is a topic that annoys both of them.

J: (stretching) So, back-to-school shopping . . . It's that time again.

M: (nodding) Yep, and we need to talk about how we're handling it this year. No surprises, José. You hear me?

J: (sighs) You're still holding last year against me, huh?

M: (firmly) José, you went way overboard with Bella's shopping last year. You told me it was just a few things, and then you sent me a text asking for wayyyyyy more than we agreed to spend. I had to pick up extra shifts to cover it, which wasn't fair to me—or my husband, honestly. It caused a lot of extra chaos in my life.

J: (raising hands in defense) Okay, okay. I get it. I got carried away. Bella was excited, and I wanted to make her happy. It was so fun at the moment and I can do it for her.

M: (leaning forward) And I want them to be happy, too, but we can't let that derail our budget. We need a plan—one we both agree on and stick to otherwise I become the bad guy.

J: (nodding slowly) All right, what's the plan?

SCRIPTS

M: (pulls out a notebook from her purse) Let's start by listing what they actually need. Bella's starting high school, so I get that she'll want some new clothes to feel confident. But Alex? He's nine—he's easy. A few pairs of jeans, some shirts, and sneakers.

J: (grinning) And maybe a hoodie or six. He loves those.

M: (smiling) Sure, two hoodies. Then there's haircuts for both and doctor's appointments.

J: (frowning) Haircuts and doctor visits—that's not my lane!

M: Yeah, I know. I can make the appointments on the days I am off in the morning from work and take them, but I'll need you to agree to stick to the budget we set for shopping.

J: (reluctantly) All right. What's the budget?

M: (flipping a page) For Bella, let's say $300 max. She'll need more since she's starting high school and wants to feel good about herself. For Alex, $150 should be enough.

J: (grinning) I can work with that. How about this—I'll take Bella shopping. It'll be our thing. I'll keep it within the budget, I promise. And . . . if I overspend it will be 100% on my dime.

M: (eyebrow raised) You're sure?

J: (mock serious) Cross my heart.

M: (laughs) Okay. And I'll handle Alex's shopping and take care of the appointments. Divide and conquer, right?

J: (nodding) Works for me.

M: Me, too.

J: (smiling). And hey, I'll try not to spoil Bella too much . . . but no promises if we see those trendy sneakers she's been talking about.

M: (shaking her head with a smile) Just stick to what we agreed, José.

End Scene

SCRIPT 13: TIME FOR A FAMILY HUDDLE

Setting: William (W) and Sophia (S) are on a Zoom call ready to talk about Stella's travel soccer opportunity, but they need to iron out logistics and finances before both parents can give it a thumbs up.

W: (smiling) Hey, Sophia. Thanks for making time for this. Stella's been buzzing about joining this travel soccer team all week. It's so great that they asked her to join.

S: (nodding) Yeah, she's pretty excited. I want her to do what she loves, but I've got some concerns we need to talk through. It's a lot of time and money.

W: (leaning forward) Yeah and . . .

S: (taking a deep breath) It's just . . . travel soccer is a big commitment. It's 30 minutes each way for practices, and that's on top of school, homework, and everything else. I'm worried about her getting enough sleep and having time for friends. Also, what about our time? It will be now devoted to driving to practices, weekends away in random cities for tournaments, I don't know if I am ready for all that.

W: (nodding) I get that. It is a lot, but you know how much Stella loves soccer. She's got real potential, and this could open doors for her. I did it as a kid and it was the best thing for me.

S: (sincerely) I know you loved it. And I want to support her, but it's not just the time—it's the cost. Gas for all those trips, tournament fees, hotel stays . . .. It adds up quickly.

W: (acknowledging) You're right. It's definitely more expensive than rec soccer. But what if I'm willing to take on most of the financial burden if that helps.

SCRIPTS

S: (raising an eyebrow) Most? Keep talking . . .

W: (smiling) Okay, I was thinking a 70/30 split. I'll cover 70% of the expenses, and you can cover the rest.

S: (considering) That's generous, William. What does the rest mean? Hotel and travel?

W: No, we can take the entire expense and then divide it up at the end of the season. If you like I can keep a spreadsheet of expenses and check in once in a while.

S: (relieved) Okay, if we can split the costs 70/30 and you take on most of the driving, I think we can make this work.

W: (grinning) Great! I'll email the coach to confirm she's in.

S: (smiling) Thanks, Will. I appreciate you stepping up for this.

W: (sincerely) Anything for Stella, my favorite girl.

End Scene

SCRIPTS

SCRIPT 14: THE GAME WITHIN THE GAME: TOURNAMENT LOGISTICS

Setting: William (W) and Sophia (S) are waiting for the soccer game to begin and start talking about the upcoming tournament schedule. Both want to support their daughter but need to iron out the details about accommodations, expenses, and time-sharing for the showcase tournament in April. For married couples this takes skill and balance of time, money, and resources; for co-parents there is an extra layer of communication and compassion sometimes needed especially in the first few years.

W: (smiling) Hey, Sophia. Exciting about the tournament, right? Stella's been talking about it nonstop.

S: (smiling back) Yeah, she's thrilled. It's a big deal for her to play in front of some scouts, and I'm glad we're both going to be there.

W: Definitely. But we need to figure out the logistics—who's covering what and, most important, where Stella's staying.

S: (nodding) Right. I know it's technically your weekend, but Stella's already told me she'd prefer to stay in my room. Girl thing and all.

W: (sighs) I figured that might be the case. She's at that age where she's more comfortable with you for this kind of thing.

S: (gently) I know it's not ideal, but I want to make this as smooth as possible for her.

W: (leaning back) Okay, if she's staying with you, I'll get my own room. But let's talk about expenses—how do we split this?

S: (pondering) The hotel's $150 a night, we will need two rooms, and we need two nights. Plus, there's gas and meals. That's $600 + gas/meals, and so on.

SCRIPTS

W: (nodding) Yeah. Should we just divide everything 50/50?

S: (hesitant) Normally, I'd agree, but since it's your weekend, don't you think it makes sense for you to cover more of it?

W: (raising an eyebrow) That's fair, but I'm already staying in a separate room because she wants to stay with you. How about we each pay for our own rooms, you can drive up with us and save on gas and wear and tear on your car, and I'll pay for Stella at the group meals. The rest we split for whichever parent she is with pays?

S: (considering) That could work.

W: (smiling) Deal. So, I'll book my room, you book yours, and we will pick you up at 2 p.m. on that Friday.

S: (smiling) Great. Can we also agree not to let her pick the music for the car ride?

End Scene

SCRIPTS

SCRIPT 15: PREPARING FOR THE LAST MILE

Setting: Averi (A) and her mom, Natalie (N), are in the car on their way home from a doctor's appointment. The mood is heavy; both are processing the implications of Natalie's health. Averi grips the steering wheel, knowing she needs to start a conversation about finances but feeling the weight of the moment.

A: (glancing at Natalie) Mom, you did great at the appointment today. I know it's not easy hearing all of this.

N: (staring out the window) Thanks, sweetheart. It's just . . . a lot to take in. I never thought we'd be here so soon.

A: (nodding) I know, and I hate that we're even having to think about this. But, Mom, we really need to talk about some important things soon—about your finances and what you'd want me to know if things get harder for you to manage on your own.

N: (hesitant) My finances? Averi, I've been handling things just fine.

A: (gently) I know you have, Mom. But you've always told me to be prepared, right? This isn't about right now—it's about making sure I can help you later if you need me to.

N: (sighs) What kind of things are you talking about?

A: (taking a deep breath) Things like where the safe is and the code for it, which bank accounts you have, and if your will is up-to-date. Just practical stuff, so I'm not scrambling if anything unexpected happens.

N: (quietly) That makes sense . . . I guess. It's just hard to think about.

A: (reaching over to squeeze her hand) I know it is, Mom. It's hard for me, too. But I don't want us to wait until it's too late to get organized.

SCRIPTS

N: (nodding) I don't want that either. So, what do we do?

A: (relieved) How about this—when we get home, let's have lunch and then sit down together to go over what we can. We'll just take it one step at a time.

N: (with a small smile) Lunch first? I like that plan. Okay, let's do it.

End Scene

SCRIPTS

SCRIPT 16: PASSING ON PEACE: THE LEGACY CONVERSATION

Setting: Ernie (E) is sitting in his quiet living room, holding his phone, while Gabe (G) is on the other end, walking home from work in the city. The conversation takes an unexpected turn for Gabe, but Ernie feels it's time to have "the talk."

G: (answering the phone) Hey, Dad! What's up?

E: (calmly) Hey, Gabe. Just thought I'd give you a call. How's work?

G: Busy, as usual, but good. Looking forward to coming home next weekend, though.

E: (chuckling) Good. Your mom's already planning your favorite meals.

G: (laughs) I can't wait. So, what's on your mind?

E: (pauses) Well, there's something I want to go over with you while you're here. It's . . . about my affairs.

G: (confused) Your affairs? What do you mean? You and mom are getting divorced?

E: (taking a deep breath) No, silly, my finances. I'm talking about my end-of-life planning, Gabe. You saw what I went through with your uncle's estate last year—digging through papers, trying to figure out what he wanted. It was a mess, and I don't want to leave you in that kind of situation.

G: (caught off guard) Oh . . . wow. I wasn't expecting that, Okay, go on.

E: (gently) I know it's not the kind of thing you want to think about, but it's important. I've been trying to put together a folder with everything—my will, passwords, account information, even instructions for what I want, and I want to sit down and share it all with you.

SCRIPTS

G: (pauses) That's . . . a lot to process.

E: (nodding, though Gabe can't see it) I get it, son. It feels weird to me too to share all this information with my kid, but trust me, it'll be better this way than you digging through my drawers.

G: (sighs) All right, Dad. If it's that important to you, we'll go through it when I'm home.

E: (relieved) Thanks, Gabe. It means a lot to me.

G: (half-joking) You're not planning to leave us anytime soon, though, right?

E: (laughs) Not if I can help it. This is just about being prepared.

G: (smiling) Okay, just checking.

E: (softly) Thanks, son. See you next weekend.

G: (smiling) Sounds good, Dad. Love you.

E: Love you too, kid.

End Scene

SCRIPTS

SCRIPT 17: SIBLING SOLUTION: NAVIGATING MOM'S NEXT CHAPTER

Setting: Averi (A) is driving home from looking at an assisted living facility when she calls her brother, Liam (L), to fill him in on what she learned. Both are committed to helping their mom, Natalie, transition into her new assisted memory care facility but need to finalize their plan.

L: (answering the phone) Hey, Averi. What's up?

A: (relieved) Hey, Liam. So glad you answered. I just left the facility I think will be the right fit for Mom, but they have a waiting list and we need to decide right away if we want to add her to the list.

L: (sighs) Okay, I guess we can't put this off much longer, huh? How's she doing?

A: (pausing) She's nervous, but she's trying to stay positive. The place is great, but the logistics and costs are . . . overwhelming.

L: (concerned) I bet. How much is it?

A: (nervously) It's going to be $8,000/month. She has enough to cover the first year, but after that, it's going to get tight. I'll be handling most of the day-to-day stuff since I'm local, but I could really use your help moving and then what do we do after her money runs out?

L: (thoughtful) What do you need me to do?

A: (smiling) Win the lottery! How about helping move her—doing the physical labor. Also, she will let you throw things away easier than when I ask her. Can you fly or drive down for a long weekend and help with that?

L: (nodding) Yeah, I can make that work. I'll take some time off and be there.

246

A: (relieved) Thank you. And for the long term, anything you can contribute financially would really help.

L: (considering) Let me look at my budget . . . For now, I think I can send $500 a month to help cover her costs.

A: (grateful) Thanks, Liam. That will help a little, but any way you can do $670? If you do, it comes to one month's rent, and I'll pay one month's rent, which will allow her to stay there a little longer till we figure something out.

L: (smiling) Let me see what I can do, but I can start with $500 for now. And I'll help with whatever paperwork or logistics you need while I'm there.

A: (nodding) That would be amazing. Mom's going to feel so much better knowing we're doing this together.

L: (warmly) She's our mom—there's no other way. Let's make her transition as smooth as possible.

A: (smiling) Agreed. Thanks, Liam.

L: (reassuring) I've got your back, Averi. See you soon.

End Scene

SCRIPTS

SCRIPT 18: SIBLING GROUP CHAT

Setting: José (J) is sitting at the kitchen table in his childhood home trying to find a way to handle his late mother's estate, including the house. He picks up his phone and starts a conversation with the sibling group chat with Ana (A) and Carlos (C).

J: Hey Ana, Carlos—planning a family dinner at Mom's house this Sunday at 7 p.m. to discuss her estate. Siblings only.

A: Hey, thanks for setting this up, but I am only coming if my husband comes. He is part of this family, too.

J: I'm sorry, Ana, but I need us to keep this discussion strictly among the three of us. Too many outside voices can complicate things.

A: But he's immediate family, too . . .

J: I get that, but for this conversation, I really need it to be just us siblings, like the old days. We can update him later if needed.

C: Agreed. We need a focused discussion and start taking some actions. I am ready to get my payout.

A: All right, just us siblings on Sunday then.

J: See you both Sunday at 7 at Mom's house.

C: Sounds good. See you Sunday.

A: Okay, see you Sunday.

End Scene

SCRIPT 19: BUT WHERE WILL I LIVE?

Setting: Sam (S) has stopped by to check in on her mom, Natalie (N), when she finds her sitting at the kitchen table lost in thought. It's been about a month since her dad has passed and Mom is struggling each day without him.

S: (cheerful) Hi, Mom, you look lost in thought. What's up?

N: (voice wavering) Sam, I keep losing sleep over this. I'm terrified I'll have to leave our home—the house we've lived in for 30 years. What if I can't afford to keep it now that Dad is gone?

S: (sincerely) I know, Mom. I feel your worry, and it breaks my heart to see you like this. But I remember when I was looking to buy a house Dad shared with me how much this house was and now I know it is worth so much more in value.

N: (with a hint of hope mixed with uncertainty) He said that, didn't he? I just can't see it right now through all this grief and uncertainty.

S: Yes, he did. And on top of that, I know he refinanced the house in 2022 when the rates were really low. That refinancing means we have built up some real equity in this place.

N: (eyes welling with tears) Equity? I never really understood what that meant. I just worry about losing our memories—losing our home.

S: (gently reassuring) Mom, equity is like a safety net. It means that if we ever needed to sell, we wouldn't just be selling our memories—we'd be getting a solid amount of money back. And even if we decide to move someday, we can use that equity to find another home. We'll sit down together, look at all the real numbers, and sort it out step by step.

SCRIPTS

N: (sniffles, taking a deep breath) I'm scared, Sam. The thought of packing up and leaving this place . . . it feels like I'm losing Dad all over again.

S: I understand, Mom. This house holds so many memories, and I know it feels like it's part of who we are as a family. But, please remember—you will always have a home. Either we keep this one, or if things ever change, we can look into finding a new place, maybe even one closer to me. We'll work through every detail together. One day at a time right now.

N: (quietly, with a small smile through tears) Thank you, Sam. I appreciate you helping me make sense of all this. It means more than I can say.

S: (firmly yet tenderly) We'll figure this out, Mom. We'll review all the numbers and options, and I promise you, you will always have a home. You're not alone in this—I'm here every step of the way.

End Scene

SCRIPTS

SCRIPT 20: BALANCE SHEETS AND INNER PEACE

Setting: The kitchen table is cluttered with papers, including a bank statement and a few bills. Sam (S) sits next to her mom, Natalie (N), who is staring at the statement with a puzzled expression. Sam takes a long deep breath, recalling her yoga class last night, and begins to explain slowly.

S: Okay, Mom, let's take a closer look at your bank statement. At the top, you see your name, your account number, and the statement period. This tells you which dates these transactions cover.

N: (squinting at the paper, voice wavering) I see my name and a bunch of numbers . . . but what exactly is a statement period?

S: (gesturing toward the top of the document) It's the time frame for which these transactions were recorded—like from the 1st to the 30th of last month. Now, look over here on the left side; this section is your account summary. Do you see where it shows the "opening balance"?

N: (nods slowly, a mix of curiosity and uncertainty on her face) Yes, it says something like "$7,000.00" there.

S: That number is what you had in your account at the very beginning of the period. Now, below that, you'll notice a list of transactions. Each line here represents money coming in or going out.

N: (leaning in, in a questioning voice) So, when a number is positive, money comes in, and when it's negative, money leaves?

S: Exactly. For example, see this line that says "direct deposit" with a plus sign? That's money you received—likely from your pension or another income source. And over here, when you see "withdrawal" or "debit," that means money was taken out of your account.

SCRIPTS

N: (eyes widening slightly as she processes the information) I see. And what about these fees? There's a line for "monthly maintenance fee."

S: (gently touching her Mom's hand for support) Those fees are charged by the bank for managing your account. They're automatically deducted from your balance. It's important to check these to make sure they're correct. Sometimes it may change depending on your balance level. Don't worry, I'll help you keep an eye on this the first few months till we learn the account type you have and fees associated with it if any

N: (sighing deeply, a note of exasperation mixed with resignation in her voice) This is all a lot to take in. I feel so dumb.

S: (softly, with a compassionate smile) I know it feels overwhelming, Mom. Let's break it down even further. Look at the bottom of the statement— that's where you'll find the "closing balance." This is the amount you have at the end of the statement period after all deposits, withdrawals, and fees have been applied.

N: (tilting her head, a flicker of comprehension in her eyes) So the closing balance is like the final tally of everything?

S: (affirming with a nod, her voice gentle yet clear) Yes, exactly. And sometimes, you might see a section for "interest earned" if your account earns interest. That shows you how much extra money you've made just by keeping your funds in the account. In a checking account it is usually a super small number, but in an investment account it could be larger.

N: (a small, hopeful smile appearing as her face relaxes) That makes sense. I think I'm beginning to see the overall picture here.

S: (reassuringly, her tone soft and steady) Take your time with it, Mom. I know these numbers and terms aren't what you're used to. We can go over each section as many times as you need. I'm here with you—step by step— every moment of the way just like the way Dad was for me for so many years. It's my turn now to be the teacher.

N: (voice quivering with gratitude and a hint of relief) Thank you, Sam. It really helps having you explain it all so clearly. I guess I just need to take it one piece at a time, just like those crazy yoga poses you try, and slow and steady I will get there.

S: (with warmth and encouragement, gently squeezing her mom's hand) Exactly, Mom. We'll keep practicing, and soon this will become more familiar. I'm proud of you for sticking with it, and we will continue to meet until you feel confident to do this on your own.

End Scene

SCRIPTS

SCRIPT 21: FROM CRISIS TO CARE: WORKING TOGETHER WHEN IT MATTERS MOST

Setting: Madison (M) and José (J) are seated across from each other in the diner where they first met years ago. The smell of coffee and pancakes fills the air, but the mood is somber. Madison fidgets with her napkin while José stares at the menu without really reading it.

M: (breaking the silence) I can't believe we're here, José. I never thought we'd be talking about putting Alex in rehab.

J: (sighs, putting down the menu) I know. It's hard to admit, but we have to do this—for him. We can't keep ignoring the signs.

M: (nodding) I just . . . I don't want him to end up like my family, José. You know how I worked so hard to leave all that behind.

J: (reaching for her hand) I know, Maddi. We'll figure this out together. First, let's talk about the cost. What have you found out so far?

M: (pulling out her phone) The inpatient programs I've looked at are about $10,000 a month. Alex is still under your insurance so we need to see what part if any they will cover.

J: (nodding) I'll call my insurance tomorrow; they are closed right now. I'll ask them what's covered, what the deductible is, and if there's an approved list of facilities.

M: (grateful) Thank you. That'll help narrow down the options. If it's $10,000 a month, and the deductible is something like $7,000 if it's the same plan you had a few years ago . . .

SCRIPTS

J: (cutting in) I'll cover $5,000 of the deductible and you can cover the rest.

M: (relieved) That's a big help. I have some money in savings and can pick up a few extra shifts to make up the difference. Then we can see how much we are responsible for after the deductible is met.

J: (thinking aloud) Maybe we can look into outpatient programs as a backup. They're less expensive but might not be enough for Alex right now.

M: (hesitant) I agree. He needs the structure and support of inpatient care. Outpatient can be the next step after he stabilizes, but right now . . . (she trails off).

J: (leaning forward) Okay, so we'll focus on getting him into inpatient care first. Let's also set up a meeting with the facility to have them share information with both of us. I can be available at lunchtime any day.

M: (nodding) And we'll need to talk to him together. I am not doing this alone! He's not going to like this, and we have to be on the same page.

J: (firmly) Agreed. We'll present it as non-negotiable. He goes, or . . .

M: (finishing his thought) Or we can't let him stay with either of us. It's tough love, José.

J: (sighs deeply) Yeah . . .

M: (softly) It is. Let's meet again after you talk to the insurance, and I'll research facilities with openings.

J: (reaching across the table) Deal. We'll get through this, Maddi. For Alex.

M: (holding his hand) For Alex.

End Scene

SCRIPTS

SCRIPT 22: THE THERMOSTAT STANDOFF

Setting: Sophia (So) and Stella (St) are sitting on the couch, facing each other. The tension is palpable as they prepare to address their ongoing disagreement about the thermostat. Sophia is holding the most recent electric bill, while Stella sits with her arms crossed.

So: (calm but firm) Stella, we need to talk about this thermostat situation. It's becoming a real issue, and I'm not going to keep fighting with you over it.

St: (rolling her eyes) Mom, it's not a big deal. I like it cooler. It's not like I'm asking for much. I just don't want to sweat sitting in the house.

So: (raising the bill) It *is* a big deal. Look at this bill. Last year, the use for this time was way lower and $75 less. You can't expect me to pay more just because you want it to feel like Antarctica in here.

St: (defensive) It's not Antarctica! It's just comfortable. I can't sleep when it's so warm.

So: (taking a deep breath) I get that. But this is *my* house, Stella. I've been paying the bills for years, and I'm comfortable with the temperature at 74. It's fair for me to stick to that since I'm footing the bill.

St: (softening) I get that, but 74 feels stuffy to me. I can barely breathe in here.

So: (nodding) Okay, let's find a compromise. We'll leave it at 74 as the default. If you want it cooler, you can pay the difference in the electric bill from last year to this year.

St: (raising an eyebrow) How would that even work?

So: (pointing at the bill) The electric bill shows use for the same time last year. If this year's usage is higher, we'll calculate the difference. You'd cover the cost of the extra electricity.

256

SCRIPTS

St: (thinking) So, I pay only if I set it lower than 74? I get it cooler and would only have to pay like $75 more?

So: Exactly. That way, you get what you want, and I don't have to carry the extra cost.

St: (reluctantly) Fine.

So: (smiling) Great. And please don't touch the thermostat without telling me first as I have a warning to put a sweater on, okay?

St: (grinning) Okay, deal.

End Scene

SCRIPTS

SCRIPT 23: ON THE RUN TO FINANCIAL HEALTH: LET'S TALK ADVISORS

Setting: Averi (A) and Isabella (I) are jogging through their favorite park on a crisp Saturday morning. The steady rhythm of their footsteps blends with light conversation as they enjoy the fresh air. Averi is clearly gathering her thoughts, preparing to open up.

A: (breathing steadily) Hey, Isabella, can I ask you something?

I: (glancing over, smiling) Sure, Averi. What's up? You okay?

A: Yeah, I'm fine. It's just . . . I mean, I'm a successful attorney, but when it comes to the stock market and investments, I'm clueless. I've been feeling really lost when it comes to managing my money and have no idea whom to trust with this conversation.

I: (laughs softly) Trust me, Averi, you're not alone. I still remember my high school economics class when I first heard about the stock market, then it was never brought up again in school or life. What's got you thinking about this now?

A: I agree—it was skipped over in our schooling and my parents never talked to me about investing. Then, I reached out to a financial advisor years ago, and they basically told me I didn't have enough money to work with them. It was embarrassing and made me want to avoid the topic altogether. Now, I'm wondering if I need someone who actually understands my situation—someone who won't make me feel small.

I: (nodding understandingly) I get it. Honestly, I work with a financial advisor who really gets me. She specializes in working with young professionals like us, breaks things down in plain language, and never makes you feel inadequate.

SCRIPTS

A: (relieved) That sounds exactly like what I need. Could you recommend her to me?

I: Absolutely. I'll send you her contact info right after our run. She's been a game changer for me.

A: (smiling, more at ease) Thanks, Isabella. I really appreciate it. I'm ready to learn and finally have my money work for me.

End Scene

SCRIPTS

SCRIPT 24: RESETTING FINANCIAL GOALS AND ADVISORS

Setting: William (W) is sitting at his home office desk, dressed casually but neatly, with a coffee mug in hand. His current financial advisors, Dan (D) and Stuart (S), appear on his screen, sitting in their firm's sleek conference room. The atmosphere is polite but slightly formal, with William aiming to address his concerns without confrontation.

W: (smiling politely) Thanks for making time to meet with me today, guys. I've been meaning to do this for a while.

D: (nodding) Of course, William. It's good to see you. What's on your mind?

W: (sipping his coffee) Well, I've been reviewing my portfolio recently, especially now that I'm thinking seriously about retirement. You know, post-divorce, my goals have shifted quite a bit.

S: (leaning forward) That's understandable. Retirement planning does come with new considerations. How can we help?

W: (pausing) As you know I moved and recently met a financial advisor who specializes in retirement planning. He's been giving me a lot of attention—asking detailed questions, sharing tailored strategies. Honestly, it's refreshing.

D: (raising an eyebrow) A retirement specialist? Interesting. Have they made specific recommendations?

W: (nodding) A few ideas. He's talked about tax-efficient withdrawals, creating a spending plan, and even ways to optimize Social Security. It made me realize those topics haven't come up much with us.

SCRIPTS

S: (calmly) Retirement planning is certainly a specialized area. But we've been managing your investments for a long time. We know your history, your family, and financial habits, which gives us an advantage in tailoring solutions for you.

W: (thoughtfully) I get that. But if I'm honest, I haven't felt that personalized attention for a while. It's like we've been on autopilot since we finished up my parents' estate, and I need to be more hands-on as I approach retirement.

D: (leaning back) That's fair feedback, Will. And we can absolutely make adjustments to prioritize your retirement goals more explicitly.

W: (looking directly at them) So how do you differ from this retirement specialist? If I'm going to stay with your team, I need to know what value you're bringing to the table.

S: (nodding) That's a great question. We take a holistic approach, considering your entire financial picture—investments, estate planning, and legacy goals—not just retirement. A specialist may focus narrowly on retirement strategies, which can be beneficial but may miss the bigger picture.

D: And because we've worked with your family for years, we bring continuity. We know the values your parents instilled and how you've evolved financially. That history can be a powerful tool in crafting plans that align with your long-term goals.

W: (nodding slowly) That makes sense. But I'll be honest, it feels like I've been the one driving the conversations lately, not you. That's what this new guy is offering—initiative.

S: (earnestly) We hear you, William. Let's commit to quarterly check-ins and more proactive planning on our end. Your concerns are valid, and we want to show you that we're still the right team for your needs.

SCRIPTS

W: (considering) Okay, let's give it a shot. But I'll still be exploring my options. I want to make the best choice for this next chapter.

D: (smiling) Completely fair. We appreciate your transparency, and we're here to prove our value to you. Let's schedule the first of those check-ins for next Friday at our office.

W: (nodding) Great—looking forward to it.

End Scene

APPENDIX

CHARACTER OVERVIEWS

Averi

Averi: Bouncing the basketball around, we find Averi outside trying to unwind from her corporate job as an attorney. She is trying to enjoy some rare downtime to help her relax as she can feel her Crohn's is starting to flare up, Averi is ready to make life changes. First, she meets her partner, Sam, moves in, and moves out. Her career is going well on the outside but inside she is struggling with the hours and lack of free time. We find Averi reaching out to her network to brainstorm shifting careers and support with finding a financial advisor, not just for herself but also for her mom. Along her journey of life, she also takes on the responsibility of caring for her mom as she begins to show signs of early onset Alzheimer's.

Gabe

Gabe: Starts out learning how to transition from being the best in school to learning how to be an adult in life. While he had a great upbringing, his parents did not teach him how to be an adult on his own. Life is rocky in

APPENDIX

the early years as he navigates a challenging job in New York City, paying high rent, and being lonely in a new city. After a while with the help of his dog, Spike, Gabe excels at work and making friends. Time passes and years later his parents now turn to him to support in their transition to aging parents and through death of his father.

José

José: The day he walked into the diner, everything changed for José. He married the love of his life and became a father to two beautiful children. Growing up in a first-generation American home, José was the oldest in a family and always carried adult responsibilities. This continued during and after his marriage. José moved back home with his mother after the divorce to save money and support her. When his mother passes away, sibling conflict occurs over the ownership of the home as there was no will left behind.

Madison

Madison: When we meet Madison, she is 19 years old, working at the local diner, living with roommates, and driving her beloved car named Cannonball. She meets José shortly after and finds out she is pregnant. Madison and José get married and work together to move into their own home and raise their two kids together. Unfortunately, this isn't a fairytale ending and life. Like over half of marriages, Madison and José end up divorced while co-parenting their children. Madison finds love again and ends up remarrying and living her best life.

Sam

Sam: Living her best life in a cute home she has recently purchased, Sam is feeling great about life especially since she started dating Averi. After a short amount of time, Averi moves in and they share a life together for several years until infidelity occurs. Sam and Averi work through how to

Appendix

separate their finances after the romantic relationship ends poorly, which they both find challenging. Not as challenging as when Sam's father passes away from cancer. Together, Sam and her mom navigate life and finances.

Sophia

Sophia: With her life ahead of her, Sophia is determined to make it in this world, as long as she doesn't have to make any decisions. She suffers from anxiety, which hampers her from making a decision because, what if it's the wrong one? Over time she learns how to work through decision-making with the help of her husband, William, and daughter, Stella. By the time Sophia and William divorce, she knows who she is as a woman in her late 40s (on most days). She is disappointed when Stella, who was a star soccer player, decides after college to travel the world. She realizes that it is her daughter's life now until she moves back home two years later. Together they navigate the world of living together as adults.

William

William: *Love* is William's favorite word. William loves his family, a total of three children between two ex-wives. He works hard, values time with his kids, and planning for his retirement. We spend time with him while he merges money, expands for a new family member, and separates money. He does this all before he moves into his over-55 community, where he learns it might be time to change financial advisors yet is afraid to seem ungrateful to his parents.

NOTES

CHAPTER TWO

1. Megan DeMatteo, "The Average American Has $90,460 in Debt—Here's How Much Debt Americans Have at Every Age," *CNBC Select*, November 14, 2023, https://www.cnbc.com/select/average-american-debt-by-age/#.
2. Credit Card Calculator, "It Will Take 9 Years and 9 Months to Pay Off the Balance. The Total Interest Is $13,689.82," Calculator.net, https://www.calculator.net/credit-card-calculator.html?balance=9%2C593&rate=22&payoffoption=1&fixedpaymentamount=200&year=2&month=0&x=Calculate.
3. Credit Card Calculator, "It Will Take 3 Years To Pay Off the Balance. The Total Interest is $241.07," Calculator.net, https://www.calculator.net/credit-card-calculator.html?balance=650&rate=22&payoffoption=1&fixedpaymentamount=25&year=2&month=0&x=Calculate.
4. Ben Luthi, Andrew Pentis, and Katie Lowery, "What Is the Average Student Loan Debt in 2024—and What Are the Impacts?," *CNN Underscored*, June 19, 2024, https://edition.cnn.com/cnn-underscored/money/average-student-loan-debt#:~:text=Average%20student%20loan%20debt%20in%20America,-As%20of%20the&text=51%25%20of%202021%2D22%20bachelor's,borrowers%20owe%20%2420%2C000%20or%20less.

NOTES

CHAPTER FOUR

1. The Currency, "Money Talks: Exploring the Questions and Answers Transforming Life, Work, and Play in America," Empower, n.d., https://www.empower.com/the-currency/money/money-talks.
2. Your Financial Therapist, https://www.yourfinancialtherapist.com/shop.
3. Emma Banks, "Is There Such a Things as Financial Intimacy?," The Maudern, n.d., https://getmaude.com/blogs/themaudern/is-there-such-a-thing-as-financial-intimacy.
4. https://www.prnewswire.com/news-releases/62-of-americans-dont-talk-about-money-according-to-new-empower-research-and-their-silence-may-come-at-a-cost-301797007.html.
5. Barri Segal, "32% of Coupled US Adults Have Cheated Financially," Credit Cards.com, January 24, 2022, https://www.creditcards.com/statistics/financial-infidelity-cheating-poll/.
6. Segal, "32% of Coupled US Adults Have Cheated Financially."

CHAPTER FIVE

1. https://pmc.ncbi.nlm.nih.gov/articles/PMC9351254/.
2. https://be.chewy.com/how-much-does-a-dog-cost/.
3. https://www.dogster.com/statistics/pet-adoption-statistics?utm_source=chatgpt.com.

CHAPTER SIX

1. US Census Bureau, "Number, Timing and Duration of Marriages and Divorces," Census.gov, April 22, 2021, https://www.census.gov/newsroom/press-releases/2021/marriages-and-divorces.html.
2. City National Bank, "How Emotions Can Influence Your Financial Decisions," n.d., https://www.cnb.com/personal-banking/insights/emotions-and-financial-decisions.html.

Notes

3. According to the Florida Academy of Collaborative Professionals (FACP), 31% of cases ended in less than 3 months, 33% of cases ended within 3–6 months, 31% of cases ended within 6–12 months, and only 5% of cases took more than 12 months.
4. Martindale Nolo, "How Long Does Divorce Take?," Lawyers.com, June 17, 2024, https://legal-info.lawyers.com/family-law/divorce/how-long-does-divorce-take.html.
5. Bryan Driscoll, "Cost of Divorce in Florida," Hello Divorce, January 21, 2025, https://hellodivorce.com/divorce-in-florida/cost-of-divorce.

CHAPTER SEVEN

1. "Average Cost of Back-to-School Shopping," Safe Search Kids, n.d., https://www.safesearchkids.com/average-cost-of-back-to-school-shopping/.

CHAPTER EIGHT

1. Brittany King, "Those Who Married Once More Likely Than Others to Have Retirement Savings," US Census Bureau, Census.gov, January 13, 2022. https://www.census.gov/library/stories/2022/01/women-more-likely-than-men-to-have-no-retirement-savings.html.
2. *Oxford English Dictionary*, "Love Bomb," n.d., https://www.oed.com/search/dictionary/?scope=Entries&q=love%20bomb.
3. "AARP Report: $28.3 Billion a Year Stolen from Adults 60+," AARP Colorado, n.d., https://states.aarp.org/colorado/aarp-report-28-3-billion-a-year-stolen-from-adults-60.

CHAPTER NINE

1. Farida B. Ahmad, Jodi A. Cisewski, and Robert N. Anderson, "Mortality in the United States—Provisional Data, 2023," *Morbidity and Mortality Weekly Report* 73, no. 31 (August 8, 2024): 677–81, https://doi.org/10.15585/mmwr.mm7331a1.

NOTES

2. Dmitry Diment, "Estate Lawyers & Attorneys in the US Market Research Report (2014–2029)," IBISWorld, Inc., September 2024, https://www.ibis world.com/united-states/industry/estate-lawyers-attorneys/4807/.
3. "10 Important Statistics About Sibling Estate Disputes," Lesser Lutrey Pasquisi & Howe, LLP, May 25, 2018, https://www.llphlegal.com/blog/2018/05/10-important-statistics-about-sibling-estate-disputes/?utm_source=chatgpt.com.

CHAPTER TEN

1. Rachel Minkin, Kim Parker, Juliana Menasce Horowitz, and Carolina Aragão, "Parents, Young Adult Children and the Transition to Adulthood," Pew Research Center, January 25, 2024, https://www.pewresearch.org/socia-trends/2024/01/25/parents-young-adult-children-and-the-transition-to-adulthood/.
2. The Pew Research Center conducted two surveys in 2023; one survey included 1,017 US adults with at least one child aged 18–34, and the other included 1,495 young adults aged 18–34 who had at least one living parent. See Minkin et al., "Young Adult Children and the Transition to Adulthood."
3. SAMSHSA, "2023 NSDUH Detailed Tables," July 30, 2024, https://www.samhsa.gov/data/report/2023-nsduh-detailed-tables.

BONUS CHAPTER

1. https://www.cnb.com/personal-banking/insights/emotions-and-financial-decisions.html.
2. Advisor Advancement Institute, "Inspiring Women by Partnering in Their Financial Growth," New York Life Investments, January 2024, https://www.newyorklifeinvestments.com/assets/documents/lit/women-and-investing/women-investing-research-report-2023.pdf.
3. https://www.fa-mag.com/news/women-need-to-lead-in-finances--consultant-says-54850.html.
4. Kristian Borghesan, "7 Proven Strategies to Win at the Great Wealth Transfer," *FutureVault*, February 7, 2024, https://www.futurevault.com/blog/7-proven-strategies-to-win-at-the-great-wealth-transfer.

ACKNOWLEDGMENTS

As an avid reader, this is one of my favorite parts of a book: to see who was involved in the writing process of the book I just read. For me now, as a writer, this is the most stressful page to write as I don't want to leave anyone out and I am sure I will; just know it was not done on purpose. I value each and every one of you who has shaped me to who I am today. This book has been a labor of love with the support of so many.

While the book is dedicated to my dad, the first person I want to thank is my mom, Carol. She excels at everything she does, showing me that there are no limits in life. While I was in high school, she worked full time as a vice president of a nonprofit organization while also going to school to get her doctorate degree, and she never missed any of my events or competitions. She set the bar high on what a woman could do with the right village. When I became a single parent to three toddlers, she jumped into our lives with the same passion to support and love us when we moved down the road. I couldn't be the mother, the woman, the business owner I am today without her by my side. THANK YOU, MOM!

ACKNOWLEDGMENTS

H.E.R.S. When I named my girls never did I expect our initials together to spell *hers* (thank you Heidi for realizing this)! It is a very fitting name for the all-girl house we live in that I now have dubbed with three teenagers "the sorority house." You all equally inspire me and drive me crazy. Our lives together are loud, bold, limitless, and loving. Thank you for supporting me on my journey of life and being patient with me while I learn how to parent and run a successful business.

H.E.R.S. Village. This is where I am afraid to miss anyone, which is why we are going to go with the entire village. You know who you are. You are my family by blood, my family by choice, my coworkers at the coffee shops, the minglers around the world, my kids' friends and their parents, the entire village . . . . You are my people who have cheered me on my toughest days and best ones. You are the ones who have jumped on planes, phone calls, and text messages at all hours of the day to listen to me cry, brainstorm ideas with, pick up a kid for me, and help me discover the better version of myself.

People come into your life for a reason, a season, a lifetime. Greg, you showed up just when I needed you to and introduced me to the world of financial therapy. Eternally grateful for that and your friendship through this journey.

Katie! Thank you for allowing me to stay in your beautiful home and explore Copenhagen to write this book, Sherina for brainstorming book titles with me, and Callie for keeping me accountable throughout the process.

To Wiley Publishing. Thank you Judith for asking me to come write a book. I am a girl who loves an invitation! Julie, for all the support in editing this book and to my book coach Marilyn, who helped me get this book off the ground. Working with you felt like a warm hug every time we met during the beginning process of writing this book, which I desperately needed.

Acknowledgments

To the Financial Therapy Association for being the profession home for me and Provisors for being the networking support that amazes me every day with the connections and support both online and in person.

To you the reader, thank you for trusting me on your journey.
This is just the beginning for us :).

Please stay in touch at www.c-yft.com.

ABOUT THE AUTHOR

Erika Wasserman is your go-to expert for all things money, emotions, and empowerment. With a finance degree from the University of Florida and a decade of consulting at IBM, she's no stranger to tackling big challenges—financial or otherwise. But it's her personal journey that truly sets her apart: marriage, raising three kids, living in three countries, navigating divorce and death, all while balancing life with a healthy mindset (on most days).

Erika's real-life experience with the emotional side of finances fuels her passion for helping others. As one of fewer than 100 Certified Financial Therapists (CFT) in the United States, and with a Financial Therapy Graduate Certificate from Kansas State University, she's not just about the numbers—she's about guiding you through financial emotions with clarity and compassion.

Talking about money should be easy and something done often, so Erika created the popular "Let's Talk Finances" conversation cards, designed to help people have deeper, more meaningful money conversations anywhere anytime; they are available on Amazon. You can also find

ABOUT THE AUTHOR

Erika on stage with dynamic speaking engagements and corporate wellness programs, making her a favorite for anyone seeking a fresh, relatable take on financial wellness.

Based in sunny South Florida, Erika is a single mom of three teenage girls and an avid traveler, having visited 47 countries and counting. She's ready to help you turn financial confusion into confidence and transform how you talk about money at various stages in life!

To book Erika for your next event, email her team at info@yourfinancialtherapist.com

INDEX

A

adult children, 179–90, 254–7

aging parents, 141–55, 242–7

all-in method, 63–5

Alzheimer's, 144

American Society for Reproductive
Medicine (ASRM), 93

Averi example

aging parents, 142, 144–5, 149–54

background information, 7

career choices, 40, 43–51

financial advisors, 194, 199–205

financial separation, 106, 115–22

overview, 263

relationships, 56, 59–60, 71, 73–86

B

baby boomers, 25

background

and combining finances, 63–4

effect of, on your money
mindset, 13

learning about money in, 21–2

beliefs, about money, 1–2

budget

creating new, after financial
separation, 113

for trips, 79

C

career choices, 39–52, 217–20

certified divorce financial analysts, 197

Certified Financial Therapists
(CFTs), 4, 197

change

due to aging, 144

during family growth, 91–5

resistance to, 195

children

adult children, 179–90

co-parenting, 125–38

cost of raising, 93–4, 128

discussing money with, 2, 142–3

involved in financial
conversations, 135

client fees, for financial advisors, 198

INDEX

collaborative divorce, 107–8

communication

about estate planning, 164–5

about money, 57–8, 209–11

in co-parenting, 126–7

during financial separation, 113–14

honest and open, 15

to navigate changes during family
growth, 91–2

with professionals, 44

co-parenting, 125–38, 236–41

cultural influences, 13

D

dating scams, 145

debt, 24–5

divorce, 105–22

author's experience of, 3–4

collaborative, 107–8

co-parenting after, 125–38

costs of, 108–9

DIY tools and apps, 197

dry promotions, 42–3

E

ECOA (Equal Credit
Opportunity Act), 64

emergency funds, 62

emotions

after a death, 170, 172

in co-parenting, 127

and estate planning, 163

and financial separation, 109–11

and money, 2

when ending relationships, 106

working with financial advisors,
196, 198

estate planning, 159–75, 248–53

evaluate practical solutions (MONEY),
16–17, 211

adult children, 186–7

aging parents, 151–2

career choices, 47–9

co-parenting, 133–6

estate planning, 170–1

family growth, 98–9

financial advisors, 203–4

financial separation, 118–19

relationships, 77–8, 85

young adulthood, 31–2

experiences, 14, 80

F

family disagreements, over estates,
164, 170

family growth, 89–102

cost of, 93–4

navigating changes during, 91–3

scripts, 225–30

fear, in estate planning, 163

fear, of judgment, 195

50/50 split method, 68–70

finances, merging, 55–86

financial advisors, 193–206

emotional impact of working
with, 196

Index

scripts, 258–62

types of, 196–7

financial confidence, 6

financial elder abuse, 146–7

financial infidelity, 112

financial intimacy, 60, 74–5

Financial Planning Association (FPA), 198–9

financial security, 6, 142

financial separation, 105–22, 231–5

financial stress, 6, 195

financial therapists, 4–5

FPA (Financial Planning Association), 198–9

G

Gabe example

aging parents, 142, 146–7, 149–55

background information, 7–8, 21

career choices, 40–3, 45–52

family growth, 90, 94–102

overview, 263–4

young adulthood, 20, 26–34

goals

defining your, 43–4

discussing in relationships, 57

financial, 6

nurturing shared, 16 (*see also* nurture shared goals)

planning for, 60–1

for trips, 79

H

home, adult children returning, 180–2

I

investing, 94–5

in vitro fertilization (IVF) costs, 92

J

José example

adult children, 180, 182–90

background information, 8

co-parenting, 126, 128–37

estate planning, 160, 163–4, 166–74

financial separation, 106, 114–21

overview, 264

relationships, 56, 58–9, 67–8, 73–83

K

Kahneman, Daniel, 196

L

"Let's Talk Finances Conversation Cards," 4–5

aging parents, 140

career choices, 38

co-parenting, 124

family growth, 104

family support, 178

financial conversations, 54, 192

financial secrets, 158

relationships, 88

lifestyle creep, 41

INDEX

M

Madison example
  adult children, 180, 182–90
  background information, 8
  co-parenting, 126, 128–37
  credit cards, 22–4
  financial separation, 106, 114–21
  overview, 264
  relationships, 56, 58–9, 67–8, 73–83
  young adulthood, 20, 26–35
make conversations comfortable
      (MONEY), 15, 211
  adult children, 183–4
  aging parents, 149
  career choices, 44–5
  co-parenting, 129–30
  estate planning, 166–7
  family growth, 95–6
  financial advisors, 200–1
  financial separation, 115–16
  relationships, 73–4, 83
  young adulthood, 26–7
men, selecting financial advisors, 198–9
mindset
  adopting a growth, 111
  and career, 41
  effect of background on, 14
  fixed, 2
  reasons to grow your financial, 6
MONEY acronym, 15–17
      see also specific items
money beliefs, 1–2
Money Mantra, 37, 53, 103, 123, 139,
      156, 176, 191, 207

Money Mindset Method, 11–18, 210–11
  adult children, 183–90
  aging parents, 147–55
  career choices, 44–52
  co-parenting, 129–38
  estate planning, 165–75
  financial advisors, 200–6
  financial separation, 115–22
  for growing a family, 94–102
  relationships, 73–86
  young adulthood, 26–36

N

nurture shared goals (MONEY), 16, 211
  adult children, 185–6
  aging parents, 151
  career choices, 46–7
  co-parenting, 131–2
  estate planning, 169–70
  family growth, 97–8
  financial advisors, 203
  financial separation, 117–18
  relationships, 76–7, 84
  young adulthood, 29–31

O

one by one (MONEY), 15–16, 211
  adult children, 184–5
  aging parents, 149–50
  career choices, 45–6
  co-parenting, 130–1
  estate planning, 167–8
  family growth, 96–7
  financial advisors, 202

Index

financial separation, 116–17
relationships, 74–6, 84
young adulthood, 27–9

P
parents
  of adult children, 179–90
  caring for aging, 141–55
  discussing money with children, 2
percentage of earning method, 71–2
physical signs, of emotional
    discomfort, 110
probate, 162
professionals, financial, 194–7
promotions, dry, 42–3

R
retirement savings, 142, 199–200

S
Sam example
  background information, 8–9
  estate planning, 160, 165–75
  financial separation, 106, 115–22
  overview, 264–5
  relationships, 56, 59–60, 71, 73–86
savings
  changing, when growing a family,
    94–5
  increased, 6
  for retirement, 142
school costs, 134–5
scripts
  adult children, 254–7

aging parents, 242–7
career choices, 217–20
co-parenting, 236–41
estate planning, 248–53
family growth, 225–30
financial advisors, 258–62
financial separation, 231–5
relationships, 221–4
young adulthood, 213–16
solutions, finding practical, 16–17 *see*
    also evaluate practical solutions
Sophia example
  adult children, 180–9
  background information, 9
  co-parenting, 126, 129–38
  family growth, 90, 92, 95–101
  overview, 265
  relationships, 56, 68–9
  student loans, 25–6
  young adulthood, 20, 26–33, 35–6
stress, reducing, 6, 195
structure, 11–12
student loans, 25–6
substance use and abuse, 182–3, 190

T
this or that method, 67–8
trips, planning joint, 79–80

W
wealth managers, 197, 198
William example
  background information, 9
  co-parenting, 126, 129–38

INDEX

William example (*Continued*)
  family growth, 90, 92, 95–101
  financial advisors, 194, 200–206
  overview, 265
  relationships, 68–9
wills, 159–75
women, selecting financial advisors, 198

Y
yes to compassion (MONEY), 17, 211
  adult children, 187–8
  aging parents, 152–3

career choices, 49
co-parenting, 136
estate planning, 171–3
family growth, 100
financial advisors, 204–5
financial separation, 120
relationships, 80–1, 85
young adulthood, 32–3
young adulthood, 19–36,
    213–16
yours, mine, ours method,
    65–6

Keep the conversation going with "Let's Talk Finances Conversation Cards" available on Amazon.

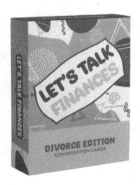 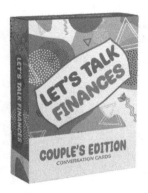

Hire Erika, Your Financial Therapist, for your next speaking engagement at info@yourfinancialtherapist.com.